The Great Commission

The Great Commission

T. Omri Jenkins

EVANGELICAL PRESS

EVANGELICAL PRESS
12 Wooler Street, Darlington, Co. Durham, DL1 1RQ, England

First published 1997

British Library Cataloguing in Publication Data available

ISBN 0 85234 390 6

By the same author:
Five Minutes to Midnight — James Stewart and mission to Europe

Printed and bound in Great Britain by
Creative Print and Design (Wales), Ebbw Vale, Gwent

To my much-valued colleagues in the European Missionary Fellowship — field workers and committee members — with gratitude for rich fellowship in the work of the gospel over forty years.

Contents

Foreword

It gives me genuine pleasure to welcome the publication of this book by my friend for over fifty years, Omri Jenkins. So I am honoured to write this brief foreword.

After he had worked for some time in the family business, the Lord brought him to saving faith and later called him to the ministry of the Word. His first pastorate in Barry, South Wales, bordered on mine in Cardiff. Some time after his summons to assume leadership of the then fledgling European Evangelistic Crusade in 1952, I was invited to serve on the executive committee, where I subsequently served as Chairman for seventeen years until my departure for Canada in 1974. This extended fellowship with Omri Jenkins brought us to a fairly intimate knowledge of each other's views and convictions. Hardly anything, except our differing understanding of baptism and some related issues, separated us. The bond has remained intact despite the geographical distance between us these last two decades. Nothing but water has ever come between us!

The foregoing facts will help to explain my pleasure at the emergence of this significant volume on the Great Commission. If you will pardon the analogy, I have experienced something akin to a husband watching his pregnant wife during the period of gestation. It has been obvious to me, especially since 1984, that something was on the way. Here is the explanation. Here is the baby! And it is no ordinary child!

It was inevitable that the mission executive should have discussed aspects of the Great Commission many times in thirty years, and heard their leader's views with growing pleasure and concurrence. Now, however, they appear before us as the developed product of mature and prolonged thought as well as of practical application in the real world of fallen men and women. When my wife, who had to read the proof pages of the book for me, reached the last chapter, a sense of awe flooded my soul. To be sure, some aspects of the book may not be beyond criticism, but few honest critics will want to deny that this is a prophetic work in a sadly unprophetic age. The writer dares to criticize what he deems to come short of God's revealed will. So, in the current moral climate, where there is no objective truth acknowledged, and no distinction of significance between 'good' and 'evil', there will be inevitable objections.

Even so, such criticism will not do anything to blunt the main thesis of this book. In fact, it will only result in placing the author in the spiritual lineage where he belongs: namely, as a modern-day representative of men like Elijah, Amos, John the Baptist and our Lord himself.

It is evident that the author had the work of evangelism, and thus of missionary outreach, primarily in mind in writing, but the rigorous method he employs makes his thesis most pertinent to other areas of life as well. One area of no less profound importance than evangelism is that of the worship of Almighty God.

It could be fairly demonstrated that what is generally referred to as the 'worship' of God has become so tampered with and tarnished that it bears scant resemblance to that which has been divinely ordained. Since what takes place in worship has the most far-reaching influence upon the whole of life, tampering with the divine model for worship casts a negative influence upon life as a whole. This tendency is a major scandal that pervades the contemporary church in all its branches, with just a few notable exceptions. We have rebelled against the dictum of an earlier age which insisted that we must worship God in God's way. In our rebellion, God is the last to be considered. Often our concern is more for providing what pleases people rather than what pleases God. This distorted reasoning, which pushes the Almighty from his rightful place and usurps what is his exclusive prerogative, ends up with the worship of self rather than of God, which is a capital sin wherever it occurs.

I refer to this particular issue because of its sinister nature and its almost universal prevalence. Omri Jenkins' robust and clear exposition both sets before us the Saviour's comprehensive plan for making disciples of the nations, and simultaneously reinforces the basis and nature of the true worship of God. May the influence of this book spread far and wide.

J. Glyn Owen
Toronto, Ontario, Canada

Preface

In 1984 I was due to share in a Missionary Conference at Knox Presbyterian Church, Toronto, where my lifelong friend J. Glyn Owen was the pastor. The theme for the conference was 'Missionary Imperatives', a subject on which I was expected to address five meetings, including two Sunday services. In the event illness prevented me from doing so and my colleague Harry Kilbride kindly deputized at short notice.

It was in preparation for that conference that I turned to the Great Commission, believing as I do that in its various parts it contains all the essential requirements for Christian mission — including divine authority, a unique message, qualified personnel, a specific aim and the means necessary for carrying out the task. What follows in this book is concerned with the outworking of these basic principles in a fallen world, which is what missionary work must always be.

Martin Luther is reported to have said, 'I did not learn my theology all at once.' That goes for me too. When I started in missionary work in 1952 I accepted the general outlook and practices of the day, but first-hand contact with missionaries, their message and methods, eventually began to raise questions and caused me to reconsider the Great Commission and the record of how it was implemented in the book of Acts, in the epistles and in the annals of Christian history. The result may be stated briefly: I had to learn some things anew and adjustments had to be made in practice. These will be reflected in the pages that follow and they are published with the hope that they will help to uphold those biblical requirements for missions in days of confusion and compromise.

I am indebted to Joan McWilliams in Welwyn for patiently transferring my pencilled scribbling to computer discs and to Bill Clark of Evangelical Press for valuable suggestions.

T. Omri Jenkins

Then Jesus came and spoke to them, saying, 'All authority has been given to me in heaven and on earth. Go therefore and make disciples of all the nations, baptizing them in the name of the Father and of the Son and of the Holy Spirit, teaching them to observe all things that I have commanded you; and lo, I am with you always, even to the end of the age' (Matt. 28:18-20).

And he said to them, 'Go into all the world and preach the gospel to every creature. He who believes and is baptized will be saved; but he who does not believe will be condemned' (Mark 16:15-16).

Then he said to them, 'Thus it is written, and thus it was necessary for the Christ to suffer and to rise from the dead the third day, and that repentance and remission of sins should be preached in his name to all nations, beginning at Jerusalem. And you are witnesses of these things' (Luke 24:46-48).

Then Jesus said to them again, 'Peace to you! As the Father has sent me, I also send you' (John 20:21).

But you shall receive power when the Holy Spirit has come upon you; and you shall be witnesses to me in Jerusalem, and in all Judea and Samaria, and to the end of the earth (Acts 1:8).

1.
An unchanging mandate

People of inquisitive minds and those preoccupied with secondary matters of interest and detail cannot but wish that the writers of the four New Testament Gospels had provided much fuller information concerning the scenes and situations in their accounts of our Lord's earthly ministry. So much could have been reported of people and places which would have made fascinating reading — the type of thing that many today would regard as being essential to stimulate and persuade readers.

If the Gospels are disappointingly short in this respect there are very good reasons why this should be so. Writing and copying manuscripts by hand was a long and laborious business, making economy in both detail and language a prime consideration. This is the implication of what we read in John 21:25: 'And there are also many other things that Jesus did, which if they were written one by one, I suppose that even the world itself could not contain the books that would be written.'

But, most important of all, the Evangelists were under the inspiration and control of the Spirit of God, who guided them to chronicle those events and utterances which revealed and attested the person of Jesus Christ, in his truly divine and truly human natures, and the efficacy of his redemptive work. This they did, without a surfeit of incidental information which might have impeded rather than facilitated their high objective.

Be that as it may, we are not prohibited from reflecting on some of those occasions in the inspired records which must have produced tensions and emotions to a remarkable degree. The repeated clashes with the powerful Jewish leaders would have been highly charged, while other occasions, such as the raising of the widow of Nain's son from his coffin, would have aroused profound emotion among what was described as a large multitude. The horrifying experience of witnessing the crucifixion was utterly devastating for all who had followed Christ, as the few words spoken by the dejected disciples on the Emmaus Road indicate, while the resurrection resulted first in incredulity and then in wondering joy. How much more of intense interest could have been written telling of all that Jesus said and did!

The appearances of the risen Christ

One could wish that the apostles' feelings, and indeed their fears, during the forty days following the resurrection had been recorded. They must have wondered what the Master's departure would mean for those who had left all to follow him. Whatever they in their ignorance had anticipated for themselves in the future, it had not included the absence of their leader. But now he had told them plainly that he was returning to his Father and, whatever they still did not understand about that, it must have meant that their own future was dark and uncertain. The fact that Peter and six others went fishing was merely the outward expression of their uncertainty, and in the circumstances we should not be too quick to condemn them.

It was on the last few occasions that the resurrected Christ was with the apostles prior to the ascension that their future was settled, when what we know as the Great Commission was specifically impressed upon them in unmistakable terms.

There appear to have been several pre-ascension situations when the Lord charged the apostles with what is summarized in the commission, though not always in the same terms. Matthew 28 speaks of a mountain in Galilee where the commission was given, while Mark 16 refers to a gathering around a table when the apostles were told, 'Go into all the world and preach the gospel to every creature.' Probably referring to the same occasion, Luke records the Lord appearing in a room in Jerusalem and there mandating the apostles to be preachers and witnesses before leading them out to Bethany where he was parted from them. Presumably Acts 1 is an extension of that final occasion. After reporting events behind closed doors on the resurrection evening, John moves on to the restoration of, and charge to, Peter at the 'Sea of Tiberias'. In all these accounts the apostles' future is in view, though the language used is different.

While none can say how many times in all the resurrected Jesus appeared to his people, it can be said that the appearances recorded in the Gospels were concerned in the main with the future role of the apostles — that is, in one way or another, with the Great Commission. Bearing in mind both the imminence of Christ's parting from the apostles and the immensity of the task committed to them, these occasions must have been affecting to a degree, no less for Christ himself than for his followers. He was returning to the Father he loved and had fully obeyed, and soon he would be seated at the Father's right hand to partake again of the ineffable glory which had been laid aside when he became incarnate. It was to be a triumphant return, for he had 'finished the work which you have given me to do' (John 17:4). He was, moreover, assured that those he was leaving behind in the world would in due time be joining him, for having 'prepared a place' for them, he would 'come again and receive you to myself, that where I am, there you may be also' (John 14:3). His last-known prayer for them had

been that 'they may be with me where I am, that they may
behold my glory which you have given me' (John 17:24). The
apostles had seen his humiliation but he knew that, by and by,
they would unfailingly gaze upon, and share in, his glory, and
this would have brought joy and satisfaction to him as he
prepared to leave them.

Yet the Lord Jesus was true man as well as true God and the
certainty of glory soon to come, and the assurance that his
apostles would ultimately share it with him, would not have
entirely dispelled the real human sorrow and regret at being
parted from those who had been his close companions for three
years. When he had first called them they had left all and
followed him; they had sat at his feet in wonderment as he had
taught them the deep things of God and prepared them for their
eventual apostolic mission. He well knew what the world
would do to them after his departure, having actually warned
them that 'The time is coming that whoever kills you will think
that he offers God service' (John 16:2). He had also given
Peter notice that ' "When you are old, you will stretch out your
hands, and another will gird you and carry you where you do
not wish." This he spoke, signifying by what death he would
glorify God' (John 21:18-19).

That such grievous forebodings must have weighed heavily
upon the Lord himself cannot be in doubt. John tells us that
'Having loved his own who were in the world, he loved them
to the end' (John 13:1). Whatever significance this statement
has for 'his own' of all ages, its first relevance was for those
in the upper room whose feet he had washed and with whom
he had shared that first Lord's Supper, the traitor Judas
excepted. Jesus loved those apostles from eternity, but he also
loved them as his earthly friends — one of them in exceptional
measure, for he is described as 'the disciple whom Jesus
loved'.

We may safely assume, therefore, that the same Lord who wept at Lazarus' grave and also over Jerusalem, as he foresaw the fate that would soon come upon it, would have been deeply affected at being parted from his chosen friends, just as they must have been at being parted from him — though we are told very little about them either. He told them not to let their hearts be troubled, but they were indeed troubled, and doubtless not a little bewildered and insecure as well. They knew their time with Jesus had been a preparation, but who of them could have imagined what it would entail? They had been an inner circle of followers to whom it had been 'given ... to know the mysteries of the kingdom of heaven' (Matt. 13:11). In other words, Christ had revealed to them knowledge not given to others. This had culminated in the ministry in the upper room when he had called them friends, telling them, 'All things that I heard from my Father I have made known to you.' And the purpose of this was 'that you should go and bear fruit' (John 15:15,16).

The commission is given

Whatever their doubts and fears, the apostles in those last hours knew the time of their graduation had come. What now remained was for the grand aim of it all to be spelt out by the Lord who had chosen and prepared them. This he did in the Great Commission, and if there were any outward manifestations of sadness and affection, these were omitted by the Evangelists to leave space for the critical exchanges concerning the task that the apostles were soon to undertake to be recorded in sharp focus. The Lord, who hitherto had been fully occupied with finishing the work the Father had given him to do, was now intent on the work which he was giving his apostles to do. The crucial point of transition had arrived wherein the great enterprise of divine redemption, in its practical outworking in the world, was passing from the Son of God to those whom he had appointed and made ready. He had been present in the heavenly council when the salvation of lost sinners had been decreed and planned and its accomplishment in time had been entrusted to, and received by, him. It was for this he had humbled himself to be born of a virgin, had lived, died and risen again from the tomb. In so doing he had secured, once and for ever, eternal redemption for every believer who will ultimately be found in heaven. It was all accomplished, complete and perfect; what remained was that the good news concerning it, the gospel, had to be carried and proclaimed to the ends of the earth. Hence the Great Commission — given first to the apostles and through them to those who would succeed them in faith and work.

That such an enterprise of grace and glory should be committed to men for any part of its fulfilment is a matter of sheer condescension and mercy. But this is what was really happening during those last hours that Christ spent with the eleven apostles prior to his ascension. The hour had come: his physical work on earth was ended; another segment of the same enterprise was about to begin. What had been foreordained in heaven and fully accomplished in Palestine was now to be borne to all nations and to every creature, and its first couriers were to be those fishermen of Galilee who had become his close companions for the last three years. What had necessarily been confined to Galilee, Samaria and Judea was now to break out from those Jewish boundaries to be freely announced to the world's multitudes, both those then living and those as yet unborn. Apparently, only five hundred or so had believed in the Saviour before he departed from this world, but within a short space of time his envoys, despite their temporary uncertainties, would see thousands saved in a single day, and these were only the first gleanings of a mighty harvest of saved souls that will eventually throng the courts of heaven when the great enterprise is complete. Did not the Master promise, 'Greater works than these he will do, because I go to my Father'? (John 14:12).

The task taken up by the apostles

In this Great Commission, then, we see the mammoth and momentous task assigned by Christ to his apostles and inevitably to all who follow in their train. The redemption which he had purchased with his own blood was, as it were, being entrusted to the apostles' care, both to be kept pure from the corruptions of men and to be proclaimed to all the world. This was not to be attempted through human ingenuity and device, as is evident from the terms in which the commission is worded, but it was none the less through them and their efforts, their faith and their fortitude. The apostles could hardly have grasped immediately all the implications of what their Lord was committing to them, but the reality and purpose of it could not be resisted, for they clearly accepted it and proceeded to wait for the promised power from heaven, without which their best endeavours would have been in vain.

Having received the commission directly from the Lord himself, the apostles necessarily became the unique custodians, as well as the first heralds, of the one true gospel. As Peter was to put it later in Cornelius' house, the apostles were 'witnesses chosen ... by God' (Acts 10:41), and it remains to their eternal credit that they did not fail either in proclaiming the gospel themselves or in passing on the charge to others, despite all opposition.

It was vital that they committed to writing what was entrusted to them because the commission had plainly been not only for them, but also for all who would believe through their word. 'All the world', 'all the nations', 'every creature' and 'the end of the age' — the Lord's plain words in the commission — clearly meant that the mandate given to the apostles was intended also for all who would follow them in every succeeding generation, literally 'to the end of the age'. What this means is that the supreme business of the church in all ages was clearly and authoritatively spelt out in unmistakable terms at the very beginning by the one who is, alone, the Head of the church. It is, and always has been, the same business and work as that which the apostles received and proceeded to obey, and just as the fulfilment of the commission was to become the hallmark of apostolic mission, so it should have continued to be that of the historic church which claims to have been founded on the apostles and their message.

The failure of the church to obey

There can be no greater cause for grief than the mournful fact that, with some heartwarming exceptions, the professing church throughout two millennia has done almost anything and everything except what was laid down in the commission and that in general it remains today a gross distortion of what the apostles were and did. Its institutions are worldly and of human origin; its forms are pretentious and garish; its leaders bear no obvious relation to the first apostolic band, and its message is as far removed from the God-centred gospel first entrusted to its original custodians as any human philosophy can be.

If a church is a company of people in succession to the apostles, worshipping the God they worshipped, owning the Lord they owned and preaching the gospel they preached, it has to be said that most of what has been, and is still being, claimed to be the Christian church is neither Christian nor the church. The sooner it all becomes one of the wrecks of time, the better it will be for the true church and the message and task committed to it by the Lord who purchased it with his own blood. The one gospel is its message and preaching it in all the world is the task entrusted to it. In these is its *raison d'être* — the reason for its existence. Failure in either therefore disqualifies a church, even though it may retain its position and power in the affairs of the fallen world.

Even those branches of the professing church which have remained closer to the apostolic pattern in both doctrine and practice have often fallen short of that pattern in so far as going into all the world and preaching the gospel to every creature is concerned. One such branch thought it 'preposterous to spread the gospel among the heathen', while another regarded evangelistic efforts as reprehensible 'enthusiasm'. Most notorious of all was the occasion when the chairman of a meeting is alleged to have told a young would-be missionary, 'Sit down, young man; if God pleases to convert the heathen he will do it without your help or mine.'

If things changed for the better after those introverted times and the Great Commission came to be taken seriously for nearly two centuries, we have now reached a period of much confusion in which, on the one hand, the commission is neglected, and even opposed, by those who regard all world religions as being of equal merit and validity, while, on the other, there are those who regard it as giving them *carte blanche* for every whimsical initiative undertaken in the name of evangelism.

If the Bible is indeed the very Word of God in written form, the infallible authority in all matters of truth and practice for his people 'to the end of the age', then this commission, in all its parts, must be heeded and obeyed, no matter what men may say or do against it. It was the Lord's final word to those he called his own, the great company of the redeemed, the church he is building and against which the powers of hell will not prevail.

Let all the redeemed of the Lord once again hear and pay heed to his last words, for the days are evil and the hour is late. 'Blessed is that servant whom his master will find so doing when he comes' (Luke 12:43).

And as they went to tell his disciples, behold, Jesus met them, saying, 'Rejoice!' And they came and held him by the feet and worshipped him (Matt. 28:9).

And when they saw him, they worshipped him; but some doubted. Then Jesus came and spoke to them, saying, 'All authority has been given to me in heaven and on earth' (Matt. 28:17-18).

And they worshipped him, and returned to Jerusalem with great joy (Luke 24:52).

For he taught them as one having authority, and not as the scribes (Matt. 7:29).

'… as you have given him authority over all flesh, that he should give eternal life to as many as you have given him' (John 17:2).

2.
'All authority has been given to me...'

The ramifications of the Great Commission for the apostles were so immense that one might wonder why they did not reject it out of hand. One of the principal reasons why they did not do so is to be found in the amazing claim with which the Lord prefaced it: 'All authority has been given to me in heaven and on earth' — a statement the implications of which the apostles had already begun to understand and accept. Matthew and Luke both report that, during those last poignant moments before Christ departed from them, 'They worshipped him' (Matt. 28:17; Luke 24:52).

The disciples' dilemma

These worshippers, we remember, were Jews who had been devout in the profession and practice of the Jewish faith which, whatever its faults and failings, was strong and uncompromising in its rejection of pagan idolatry. The worship of one God was its chief distinguishing feature; this was what separated the Jews from superstitious Gentiles, who commonly worshipped anything from a wooden pole to the Roman emperor. True, their worship of the true God was flawed for one reason or another, as the New Testament makes plain, yet the one they worshipped was the God revealed in the Old Testament. Besides Jehovah, there was for the Jews none other, and he was the transcendent Deity who could not be represented by any image and was altogether separate and different from man. Their Scriptures forbade them thinking of him in any human terms, either physically or philosophically: 'For as the heavens are higher than the earth, so are my ways higher than your ways, and my thoughts than your thoughts' (Isa. 55:9).

It was inconceivable, therefore, that God could be thought of as man in any respect, and still more so that a man could possibly be God. This had been the vital issue, the sticking-point, for the Jewish leaders throughout Christ's public ministry, namely that he was 'making himself equal with God' (John 5:18). When he appeared before the Sanhedrin, it was the last straw that he should claim to be the Son of God and say, 'Hereafter you will see the Son of Man sitting at the right hand of the Power, and coming on the clouds of heaven' (Matt. 26:65). For monotheistic Jews this was the ultimate blasphemy, punishable by death.

To believe in Jesus of Nazareth as the Son of God must therefore have been extremely difficult for Christ's disciples, which is probably the reason why only one pre-resurrection account of them worshipping Jesus is recorded in the Gospels. This was when they glimpsed something of his divinity when he walked on the water. Others had worshipped him after miraculous healings. But, though real and powerful, these had been only brief encounters, whereas the disciples were living daily with one who was in every respect a true man like themselves, subject to thirst and hunger, fatigues and feelings, even as they were. For Jews such things would have been unthinkable in the God of Old Testament revelation. The truth that God had become man in the person of Christ was to become the chief cornerstone of the gospel of which the disciples were soon to be the first heralds to the world, but that was not until after the resurrection had declared him to be 'the Son of God with power'. Until then questions and doubts concerning Christ must inevitably have assailed them, especially when, after they had confessed him to be 'the Christ, the Son of the living God', he began to warn them of his impending sufferings and death. 'This shall not happen to you!' Peter had exclaimed in horror (Matt. 16:16,22).

The dilemma Peter and his fellow apostles must have felt was simple and straightforward: how could Deity die? How could God the Son be abused by men and killed? If they believed one minute and doubted the next, this was understandable in men with their religious background. Because of that background, too, Christ's way with them was to teach and lead them patiently to that unshakeable knowledge of him that would make them true worshippers. It was after his resurrection that this was achieved; 'doubting' Thomas's confession when he had seen and touched the risen Lord is eloquent beyond measure: 'My Lord and my God!' (John 20:28). Yet while Thomas and other apostles 'worshipped him', and thereby signalled that he was none other than God manifest in the flesh, the one who was 'full of grace and truth', Matthew notes that 'some doubted' still (Matt. 28:17) — which only demonstrates the perplexities that devout Jews would have felt and, of course, have felt ever since.

The authority of Christ

Having finally and unequivocally known Jesus as God the Son and worshipped him as such, the apostles were able to perceive the significance of, and to accept, the assertion which the Lord

made in the preface to the Great Commission: 'All authority
has been given to me in heaven and on earth.' There were two
important reasons for this assertion of authority — one being
the magnitude of the commission itself, and the other its
implications for them in terms of what their future obedience
to it would require.

There is a parallel here, in meaning if not in actual words,
with the Lord God manifesting himself to Moses in the bush
that burned but was not consumed. Moses had to remove his
sandals before being charged with leading captive Israel out of
the Egyptian brickfields. Moses' action in removing his sandals to stand on holy ground before God is not unlike the
response of the apostles as they worshipped the Lord Jesus.
Moses, moreover, had need for an authority greater than any
that he himself could muster, in order to deal with Israel as
much as with Pharaoh. 'What shall I say to them?' he asked.
The Lord replied, 'Thus you shall say to the children of Israel,
"I AM has sent me"' (Exod. 3:13,14).

The one who called himself 'I AM' on Mount Hebron was
the same Lord whom the disciples worshipped on the Mount
of Ascension and he was exercising the same authority for the
accomplishment of his own will and purpose. It was an
authority invested in him by God the Father for the economy
and work of redemption. As God the Son he was co-equal with
the Father in all attributes pertaining to deity, but when he
undertook to become the Saviour of lost sinners he was given
special authority in heaven and on earth for whatever that work
would entail. Before the foundation of the world of lost
sinners, he was the Lamb slain for their salvation, all authority
concerning them having been committed to him. To this he
alluded in his high-priestly prayer: '... as you have given him
authority over all flesh, that he should give eternal life to as
many as you have given him' (John 17:2).

In the exercise of that authority, he came into the world as man and displayed it in so many ways in his public ministry. Taking Luke 8 as a sample, we see the wind and waves being subject to him and the demons of Gadara too. The latter sought his permission to enter the swine and he permitted them, thereby showing his authority over the infernal regions and its denizens. The man enslaved to Satan and sin was set free by his authoritative word and his response was to sit at Jesus' feet. Wind and waves, disease and death were all subject to his authority, for he stilled the storm and the woman touching the hem of his garment was instantly healed, while Jairus' daughter was raised to life by his word.

His teaching also demonstrated the same thing: 'For he taught them as one having authority, and not as the scribes' (Matt. 7:29). When he told Nicodemus, 'You must be born again,' and went on to say that 'God so loved the world that he gave his only begotten Son, that whoever believes in him should not perish but have everlasting life,' it was with the authority of one who could say, 'We speak what we know and testify what we have seen' (John 3:7,11,16). The perverseness of fallen humanity is to believe John 3:16 in some measure while rejecting the identity and authority of the one who uttered it!

A sobering indication of the same sovereign authority of Christ was his unerring knowledge of the human heart. To the self-righteous Pharisees he applied Isaiah's prophecy: 'These people draw near to me with their mouth, and honour me with their lips, but their heart is far from me' (Matt. 15:8). He knew too the duplicity of those who questioned him asking, 'By what authority are you doing these things?' and exposed it in no uncertain way (Matt. 21:23-27). Most telling of all were his dealings with some who professed to believe 'in his name when they saw the signs [miracles] which he did'. He knew they were merely dazzled by the signs but were blind to what they signified. He knew their hearts and 'did not commit himself to them, because he knew all men' (John 2:23,24). They claimed to believe in him but he did not believe in them!

It was with that very same authority that he gave his life on the cross: 'No one takes it from me, but I lay it down of myself. I have power [authority] to lay it down, and I have power to take it again. This command I have received from my Father' (John 10:18). Men, in their blind hatred, nailed him to the cross, but the reality was that he, with the authority given to him, was actively laying down his life for his sheep.

Commentators suggest that after completing his redemptive work Christ was given a new authority, quoting in confirmation Philippians 2:9-11: 'Therefore God also has highly exalted him and given him the name which is above every name...' Was this something new given to him which he did not previously have, or was the reality of what had already been given him made more plain and glorious? Whatever the precise interpretation, it was in the exercise of that sovereign authority that he committed to his chosen apostles the monumental task of taking the gospel to the world. And they, having worshipped him with unclouded eyes, could not but accept the charge and prepare to obey it in the prescribed way.

Worship precedes witness

There is here, as elsewhere in the Scriptures, an evident order, the significance of which could hardly be overstated. Jesus first brought the apostles to know him in truth and to behold his glory and power, and only then did he commission them with the work of evangelizing the world. It was the same order with

Moses, and there are many other examples of it in the Word of God. Gideon, the craven farmer, was to become the liberator of his people, but not before he had seen and known the Lord and his power in the fire consuming the food set out on a rock. 'Alas, O Lord God!' he exclaimed. 'For I have seen the Angel of the LORD face to face' (Judg. 6:22). Soon he was scattering the enemies of God and of Israel. King David had known his God's deliverance from the lion and bear before he faced Goliath with five pebbles and a sling (1 Sam. 17:34-37). Isaiah 'saw the Lord sitting on a throne, high and lifted up' before crying, 'Here am I! Send me' (Isa. 6:1,8).

The same order is seen with Saul of Tarsus, for whom the encounter with the Lord on the Damascus road, and subsequently in Arabia, was the indispensable prelude to his appointment as the apostle to the Gentiles. When years later he appeared as a prisoner before King Agrippa, he described what had happened to him and its outcome: 'Therefore, King Agrippa, I was not disobedient to the heavenly vision' (Acts 26:19).

These and other biblical examples which could be adduced reflect the same essential pattern which was so significant in the way Jesus dealt with the apostles. Their minds having been convinced, their affections won and their wills yielded, the Great Commission was delivered to their care. They were, in the world's estimation, both then and ever since, a lowly breed of men, as God's servants often are — fishermen of Galilee and collectors of taxes for Rome, neither educated in rabbinical schools nor sanctioned by the religious powers of the day, but their enemies perceived that 'They had been with Jesus' (Acts 4:13). Something of Jesus had, as it were, 'rubbed off' on them. They had known and worshipped him as Lord and God and now declared his words to be the words of God himself, which had to be heeded and obeyed: 'Whether it is right in the sight of God to listen to you more than to God, you judge. For we cannot but speak the things which we have seen and heard' (Acts 4:19-20).

If the Great Commission was intended for the church in all ages — and we shall consider this in more detail later — it would have been well if the same order had always prevailed in the continuing fulfilment by the church of its God-given task in the world. What church history shows, however, is men ignoring God's way and substituting their own ways, ranging from a spurious church replete with sacraments, idols and a 'salvation' which is in truth no salvation at all, to the high-profile mass evangelism and high-decibel 'celebrations' of the late twentieth century. But even in circles where these and other man-centred aberrations are firmly eschewed, much mischief has resulted when misguided zeal has outrun the knowledge of, and submission to, the Word and will of him who is the sovereign Lord of the church.

It is a simple but serious fact of life that like produces like, as much in the realm of religion as in other realms. This is why any deviation from biblical truth and practice has inevitably resulted in still more deviations. Where Christ and his authority are held in disregard, or are merely taken for granted, moribund religion and manmade substitutes will be the vogue and a lifeless form of Christianity will ensue. Nor is a rigidly pursued dead orthodoxy any improvement; theoretical notions of God and his saving grace in Christ are no alternative to knowing the Lord of glory and obeying him in preaching the gospel to sinners. True religion is more than mere notion — more than mere belief and good intentions too; it is the Lord of heaven and earth revealing himself by grace to men and women, first that they might be saved and become worshippers in spirit and in truth, and then, as worshippers, that they should be witnesses to him and his salvation. From Abel and his offering onwards it has always been thus. The glorious visitor's message to Daniel was that, in the coming world upheavals, 'The people who know their God shall be strong and carry out great exploits' (Dan. 11:32).

Thus it was for the apostles also; they had those faculties which separate men from the animal world — mind, affections and will, all of which were necessarily employed in worshipping. Their minds were enlightened to see and know Jesus as the Son of God; their hearts' affections were fixed upon him; they really loved him; and their wills were no longer their own, but his. They worshipped him and he, with heavenly authority, sent them to share with the world what they had seen and known. 'You shall be witnesses to me,' said their Lord and King and they, having become true worshippers, obeyed his command. Shortly afterwards, they found many converts becoming worshippers like themselves: 'Continuing daily with one accord in the temple, and breaking bread from house to house, they ate their food with gladness and simplicity of heart, praising God and having favour with all the people' (Acts 2:46-47).

Sadly, the essential element in true worship is not all that conspicuous in late twentieth-century Christendom. While some sections are taken up with a spurious priesthood, both male and female, which they regard as essential for worship, others are convinced that worship is a free-for-all of sound and action, while yet others conceive it to be a matter of rigid traditional practice. What appears to be common to us all is the absence of a real awareness of God and of capitulation to the one who is Lord and King, with all authority in heaven and earth in his hand.

It is said that a defeated admiral, advancing with outstretched hand in surrender to Nelson, was curtly told, 'Not your hand, your sword!' True worshippers are not only believers; because of that encounter with him who is Lord of all, they have yielded up their sword to him. They worship and adore him; they 'bring forth the royal diadem and crown him Lord of all'.

The need for gospel missions at home and abroad has never been greater or more urgent. But neither the enormity of the need nor the urgency of the task should be allowed to subvert the biblical pattern of being worshippers first, and then witnesses. It is 'the people who know their God' who 'shall be strong, and carry out great exploits'.

Go therefore and make disciples of all the nations
(Matt. 28:19).

Go into all the world and preach the gospel to every
creature (Mark 16:15).

Then he appointed twelve, that they might be with him and
that he might send them out to preach (Mark 3:14).

You did not choose me, but I chose you and appointed you
that you should go and bear fruit (John 15:16).

As you sent me into the world, I also have sent them into
the world (John 17:18).

Then Jesus said to them again, 'Peace to you! As the Father
has sent me, I also send you' (John 20:21).

3.
'Go into all the world...'

Some commentators emphasize that it is the participle *'going'* which is used by both Matthew and Mark in their summaries of the Great Commission, rather than the imperative 'Go!' found in most English versions. This implies that the apostles knew before receiving the final commission that they would be *going* because of what the Lord had already shown and told them during their period of discipleship. Moreover they must have been profoundly impressed with what they had seen of Christ himself. He had always been *going* — from Galilee to Samaria and Judea and back again; to the Decapolis region in the east and the borders of Sidon on the west; always doing the will of the one who had sent him, even though he was sometimes overcome by fatigue while doing so. These apostles had trailed in his wake, often equally tired and sometimes impatient with his forbearance with the crowds who were constantly besieging him.

John the Baptist's ministry seems to have been confined to areas beside the River Jordan, and people 'went out to him'; but the one who was mightier than John traversed city streets and country roads, crossed and recrossed Galilee's lake, attended synagogues and temple feasts — all in the task of seeking and saving lost souls. There had been a holy restlessness about him as he resolutely pursued 'the works of him who sent me while it is day,' because 'The night is coming when no one can work' (John 9:4). Hence, whatever their reticence and doubts, his chosen followers must have concluded that his ministry involved a *going* that required dedication and untiring effort and, whatever the future held for them, this *going* would be a part of it.

But the Lord had also illustrated his own ministry in the parables of the lost coin and lost sheep, both of which had stressed a vigorous and persevering search for what was lost until it was found. This is what his ministry really was and it was costing him his all. By implication, it was what he would require of them, for he told them, 'If anyone desires to come after me, let him deny himself, and take up his cross, and follow me' (Matt. 16:24). He had more than once sent them on evangelizing expeditions, sending them forth without 'money bag, sack, nor sandals', and had said they were his friends whom he had chosen to go and bear fruit. And in his high-priestly prayer he declared, 'As you sent me into the world, I also have sent them into the world' (John 17:18).

Even more significantly, part of the upper-room ministry had been to warn them of what they would face in due time: 'The time is coming that whoever kills you will think that he offers God service' (John 16:2). This is what their future life and work would involve.

There can be no question, then, but that during their discipleship days the apostles were clearly shown by constant example, taught by vivid parables and told in plain words that they would eventually be *going* to the world, and the Great Commission would, therefore, have come as no surprise to them. If doubts and apprehensions remained, they would have been concerned with precisely what their mission was to be and where it was to be pursued. The commission spelt it all out. The specific task, its scope and aim were all explicitly laid down, and the apostles could not fail to understand, if indeed they had not already done so in some measure, that their future work was to be nothing less than a continuation of what they had seen with the one they now worshipped.

'Beginning at Jerusalem...'

With the inspiration of Christ's resurrection, the express instructions in the commission and the enduement of power at Pentecost, the apostles could have been expected to obey all that was laid down for them, and to do so with alacrity. Yet they seem to have dragged their feet in one respect. While they went and preached to their fellow-Jews without delay, there appears to have been some reluctance to reach out beyond the frontiers of Judaism. That part of the commission which defined their field of operations as 'all the nations', 'all the world', 'every creature', and 'to the ends of the earth' was initially left in abeyance, either through preoccupation or prejudice, or possibly a mixture of both.

Before we, from our late vantage-point, begin to sit in judgement on the apostles, we would do well to try to appreciate the scene in the days following Pentecost, with its all-pervading Jewish ethos, its deep-rooted historic traditions and its narrow but powerful nationalism, all of which was anchored to the monotheistic religion revealed to their forefathers and carefully maintained by their Scriptures. In stark contrast to this, and in close proximity because of the dominating presence of the Roman Empire and its armies, were the gross superstitions and immoral excesses of paganism.

Furthermore, it was the womb of the Jewish nation that had given birth to the Lord himself and through him to the faith the apostles now professed and preached. The ascended Lord had in the flesh been a fellow-Jew and he had owned the God of Abraham, Isaac and Jacob as his Father and had taught that everything that he was and did was in fulfilment of the Jewish Scriptures. By word and deed he thus enhanced the authority and influence of those Scriptures for the apostles and their converts.

But, probably most significant of all in this connection, the remarkable success attending their first efforts at Pentecost and in the days that followed was among Jews in Jerusalem, Judea and Samaria. This inevitably would have made heavy demands upon the apostles and would have allowed little thought for 'all the world' beyond, even if the desire to obey the commission fully was still present with them.

Be all that as it may, it can be seen that the apostolic church was in danger of developing into the mere outcrop of Judaism which some at first perceived it to be. As the Acts of the Apostles and the epistle to the Galatians show, the Judaizing Christians, with their insistence on circumcision being necessary for salvation as well as faith in Christ, would have realized that perception, and turned the historic Jewish framework into a strait-jacket for the new-born church and its faith.

'To all nations'

It was divine intervention, both direct and providential, which finally freed the gospel from the matrix of Judaism and brought 'all the world' into focus for the apostles and other believers. The death of godly Stephen, for more reasons than one, must have seemed disastrous for the young church, but in retrospect it can be seen to have been the death-blow for overweening Judaism. Stephen condemned his fellow-Jews for being 'stiff-necked and uncircumcised in heart and ears' (Acts 7:51). But he also shattered the prevailing bondage to the temple which may still have affected apostles and believers: 'The Most High does not dwell in temples made with hands, as the prophet says: "Heaven is my throne, and earth is my footstool"' (Acts 7:48-49). That this had some effect is suggested by Paul's use of the same words on Mars Hill in Athens a few brief years later. It must have influenced others as well, if only in confirming them in holding their meetings in houses and other places.

Even more important, Stephen's martyrdom sparked off outright persecution, as a result of which many 'were scattered' and 'went everywhere preaching the word' (Acts 8:4), and it was some of these nameless Christians who witnessed to Gentiles in Antioch and were thus used to found the first non-Jewish church, which was soon to become the launch-pad for Gentile missions (Acts 11:19-26; 13:1-3).

But Luke is careful to report two other vital details in his account of Stephen's death: one was that 'The witnesses laid down their clothes at the feet of a young man named Saul' (Acts 7:58); and the other that 'Saul was consenting to his death' (Acts 8:1). It is almost certain that what Saul heard and saw that day became one of the goads that the Lord used to prepare him, first for conversion, which was not long in coming (Acts 9:5), and, secondly, for the ministry he was to pursue as the apostle to the Gentiles. The blood of the first Christian martyr became the seed of the world church.

The next step in the escape of the gospel from its Jewish moorings was God's gracious dealings with the Gentile Cornelius and with Peter, the striking result being that the apostle to the Jews became the first to preach to a Gentile group and in a Gentile home. The enormity of this step is reflected in the fact that Peter had to defend his action to the Jewish believers, saying, 'Who was I that I could withstand God?' (Acts 11:17).

Meanwhile, the converted Saul of Tarsus had been in Arabia, there receiving from the Lord himself the gospel he was to proclaim (Gal. 1:17) and after eventually visiting

Jerusalem he returned to his native Tarsus. While he was there the nameless Christians who had been scattered from Jerusalem following Stephen's death arrived in Antioch and, if some still only testified to Jews, a few of them turned to speak to the Gentiles who made up most of the population of what was the fourth city of the Roman Empire, a pagan capital and a prosperous trading-centre. Such was the blessing attending their efforts that 'A great number believed and turned to the Lord' (Acts 11:21). It was not long before Barnabas, delegated to Antioch by the apostles, had fetched Saul from Tarsus and under their joint ministry a great church was established, from whence they were shortly led by the Spirit to take the gospel to the Gentile world yonder.

These developments, so carefully marshalled and recorded by Luke in the book of Acts, cannot be other than the work of God, intervening directly in some of them and overruling the affairs of men in others — and all to bring about full obedience to the Great Commission. Old Testament prophets had spoken of the Gentiles coming to the light of the knowledge of God, but for the Jews the only hope for Gentiles was that they should become Jews, which many did. It is, however, still surprising that those commanded by the Lord himself and endued by his Spirit at Pentecost should have been so slow, if not actually averse, to take the gospel out of its native Jewish soil to the Gentile world and that it took divine agency to urge them to do so.

What is recorded of the early church is not merely for information; it is also for instruction and exhortation, as much for us in the late twentieth century as for any generation of Christian believers. In some real senses it should be easier for us to understand and obey than it was for the early church. Our heritage is Christian, not Jewish, and it includes accounts of our fathers in the faith taking the gospel to the world; they should be our examples and inspiration. But we have the written New Testament too, with its infallibly recorded words of our Lord and Saviour. The good news of his virgin birth was to be 'to all people' (Luke 2:10), and his forerunner described him as 'the Lamb of God who takes away the sin of the world' (John 1:29). He himself said that 'God so loved the world ... that whoever believes in him should not perish but have everlasting life.' He also said, 'I am the light of the world' (John 8:12) and 'The field is the world' (Matt. 13:38). If Israel alone was the perspective of the Old Testament, that of the New Testament is the world, and nothing can be allowed to cloud or reduce that fact.

This worldwide embrace of the gospel, so explicit in Christ's final orders to his apostles, could not have had only them and their own generation in view. Total implementation of the commission was a physical impossibility for them, for Christ promised, 'Lo, I am with you always, even to the end of the age.' The last apostle was dead before the end of the first century and only a part of the Roman Empire had been reached by then. The only possible understanding of the commission is that it was first for the apostles, as the founders of the Christian church, and through them for the church itself in every succeeding generation. The 'going' is for all who believe until the end of the age.

Hindrances to evangelism

Yet it is far from true that every age of the church has obeyed. Many malign factors and influences have combined to cut the nerve of evangelism in Christian history — some, if not all of them, the devices of Satan, for the spread of the gospel means contraction for his kingdom of darkness. The rise of heresy has always turned the church in on itself, with the purity of the faith becoming a battleground and world mission left in limbo.

Persecution, craving for power, false doctrines, complacency — all have held sway at one time or another, often to the paralysis of evangelism and missions. And recovery has come after further divine interventions in revivals, when God's people, awakened and renewed, have seen the world scope of the gospel and have felt anew the force of the Great Commission and the authority of the one they worship as Lord and God.

With the second half of the twentieth century other impediments to world mission have arisen. Ecumenism has gained ground and momentum, even promoting multi-faith worship in its hollow quest for unity. Having begun in 1910 as a movement designed to advance the spread of Christianity in the non-Christian world, it has become a monster of infidelity and an enemy of all who seek to obey the Great Commission. In brief, ecumenism, whatever its origins, has become the very negation of supernatural Christianity, as it looks to gather into a so-called 'world church' those heathen multitudes to whom God's people are expressly sent to make disciples. Should ecumenism succeed in its grandiose aim, gospel missions in the world would be proscribed as unwarranted and prejudicial to the success of the movement. The command to 'Go...' will none the less remain valid for the true church of Christ.

Aggressive humanism, with its influence on anthropology and sociology, is also challenging the very concept of converting heathen peoples to faith in Christ. Devoid of any faith of their own, humanists of various ilks claim there is no difference between what any people believe and practise and what Christianity is and does. All religions and their cultures are regarded as mere superstitions, as are their practices, which are said to have evolved over long years and to have cast their spell on successive generations within their respective spheres. To claim, therefore, that Christianity is fundamentally different from, and superior to, all other religions is, for humanists, not to be tolerated in the modern world of advanced knowledge and achievement. Now that God and the spiritual world have been finally shown to be mere superstition, the only permissible mission is that of relief for disease, famine and dire poverty. While many arguments can be deployed against such reasoning, our ultimate answer must be that Christ has saved us and has commanded us to share the good news of him and his salvation with all the world's nations, remembering, as always, that 'The natural man does not receive the things of the Spirit of God, for they are foolishness to him; nor can he know them, because they are spiritually discerned' (1 Cor. 2:14).

Possibly the most insidious hindrance of all to evangelism is the heresy of universal salvation, so long the darling of modernist theology and now the general assumption of popular Christendom. Its most devasting effect, among others, is to cut the nerve of evangelism and of foreign missions. If, one way or another, all humanity is ultimately to be saved, preaching the gospel for the salvation of souls is a waste of time, for all will be saved anyway, whether they know and believe the Christian gospel or not. The real mission is to relieve those in famine, heal the sick and generally help all in extreme poverty and crude living conditions to achieve material well-being. It is a well-known fact that some missionary societies, which were established for evangelism and church-planting, are now mere social relief agencies, and this is very largely the result of the unscriptural doctrine of universal salvation.

If these and other strong factions and influences are serious impediments to world evangelization, greater problems still are to be found within the church, rather than without. Material prosperity among Christians, which could have been expected to boost evangelistic and missionary endeavour, seems to have had the opposite effect. A prosperous self-security and contentment appear to have enervated professing Christians, who have found it easier to support professional mass-evangelism rather than get up and go themselves in local church evangelism. This may also be the reason, at least in part, for the kind of innovative short-term, superficial missionary work which is now so much in vogue, while the number of lifelong missionaries is in decline. It is a sobering fact that former times of poverty and great practical disadvantages among Christians seem to have produced more and better missionaries than later times of plenty and their much-vaunted benefits!

A neglected commission

Nor has the recovery of reformed doctrines over the second half of the twentieth century led to any marked growth in missionary and evangelistic zeal. Two centuries ago, William Carey's burning concern for the heathen world met with hyper-Calvinistic coldness and rebuff; if in this respect things are not as bad today, they are not much better either. Many of the great missionaries and evangelists of history have been Calvinist in beliefs: their strong, biblical doctrines inspired them to unswerving obedience to the Lord's commission and these same doctrines should do no less for all who share them today. Electing love and particular redemption have world relevance; otherwise the Great Commission would never have been given. To believe in the former and to neglect the latter must therefore be a contradiction of both.

Whatever the reasons, the 'going' factor, so prominent in the example and commands of the Head of the church, is far from paramount in our modern churches, reformed or otherwise. Rather let some go for exciting short-term excursions: let the 'going' be done through technology, world-televised campaigns, or radio, and let help towards the expenses be provided! The finest world maps and detailed information to hand have made world holidays, if not world missions, very attractive, even among many Christians, and the end result is that the church is often static, well-heeled and enjoying good fellowship, but so far as 'making disciples of all nations' is concerned, merely marking time and 'going' nowhere. But let it be noted by all who care that the Lord whom we worship, and to whom all authority in heaven and earth has been given, has not withdrawn his commission; it remains 'even to the end of the age'. If the true church at the end of the twentieth century will not heed that commission, it may well be that the Lord will do yet another 'new thing' to fulfil his purposes in salvation.

I will declare the decree:
The LORD has said to me,
'You are My Son,
Today I have begotten you.
Ask of me, and I will give you
The nations for your inheritance,
And the ends of the earth for your possession'
(Ps. 2:7-8).

For the earth will be filled
With the knowledge of the glory of the Lord,
As the waters cover the sea
(Hab. 2:14).

They will come from the east and the west, from the north
and the south, and sit down in the kingdom of God
(Luke 13:29).

Now those who were scattered … travelled as far as
Phoenicia, Cyprus and Antioch preaching the word
(Acts 11:19).

'… through whom we have received grace and apostleship
for obedience to the faith among all nations for his name'
(Rom. 1:5).

4.
'To the end of the earth'

It is self-evident that the Great Commission was addressed first to those apostles who had been sovereignly chosen by Christ and then specifically prepared over the three years of their discipleship. It all culminated in the post-resurrection appearances when 'He opened their understanding, that they might comprehend the Scriptures', and what they foretold of the Messiah's death and resurrection (Luke 24:45-48). Their time with the Lord and all they had seen and heard had been the necessary training for the commission which they were the first to receive.

It is equally self-evident that the commission was not for them alone. The expressions 'all the world', 'all nations' and 'the end of the age' clearly meant that the commission was intended for the successive generations of Christians in the world. Unlike what is so common in our culture, the Lord Jesus did not use language loosely; in fact he had expressly taught his followers to 'Let your "Yes" be "Yes" and your "No", "No"' (Matt. 5:37), and he was certainly careful that it should be so with him. We can use 'world' today when we really mean a wide, indefinable area, and 'all nations' for a few countries beside our own. It was not so when Jesus commissioned the apostles; 'all the world' meant the entire inhabited earthly sphere, and 'all the nations' included every ethnic group in

every continent. Hence, when telling the apostles 'that repentance and remission of sins should be preached in his name to
all nations', he added, 'beginning at Jerusalem' (Luke 24:47).
It was to begin with them in Jerusalem, but it would 'be
preached in all the world as a witness to all the nations' (Matt.
24:14) before the end of the age (cf. 'to the end of the earth',
Acts 1:8).

It may seem obvious, but it cannot be emphasized enough
that Christ was addressing every succeeding age of his church
in the commission. The fact that his professing people have
often failed to heed him, and are still doing so, neither blunts
his charge nor blights his purpose. The commission endures
unchanged, as relevant for his believing church after nearly
two millennia as any other aspect of 'the faith which was once
for all delivered to the saints' (Jude 3). The commission, in
precisely what it says and requires, is the one great business of
the Christian church in the world. If the church fails in this,
nothing else can make good the failure.

The example set by the early church

There can be no real excuse for such failure for two reasons:
first, because of all that is implied in the commission; and
secondly, in the light of the way it was worked out in the New
Testament church, which is, of course, our one and only
reliable example. There we see that the apostles were soon
joined by others, many of them nameless, who planted the
gospel in several regions without direct apostolic help. Who,
for instance, took the gospel to Italy? When Paul the prisoner,
on the last lap of his historic journey to Rome, reached the port
of Puteoli, he found brethren there and was invited to stay with
them for seven days (Acts 28:14). Similarly, Christians in
Rome heard that Paul was coming and 'came to meet us as far

as Appii Forum and Three Inns' (Acts 28:15). The fact that the gospel had reached these other places within a generation is clear evidence that the church in its earliest days took the Lord's commission seriously. Despite every hindrance the believers, wherever they were located, became part of the vigorous movement to 'preach the gospel to every creature'.

In this movement an order soon became necessary as the expanding work outgrew the scope and abilities of the apostles. It was not long before the apostles who had been set apart by the Lord were themselves setting apart others like Barnabas and Timothy to assist them in the work and it was inevitable that in due time the churches themselves would be required to appoint men whom God had called from their own ranks to preach the Word among them and wherever the Lord should lead them. Epaphras, Epaphroditus, Tychicus and others named in the New Testament may well be among them.

What a calling it was for the early Christian church to take the gospel to the world of rank paganism at a time when Christian verities and virtues had yet to take root in any real measure! The New Testament had not yet been written, which meant that, except for parts of the Old Testament which may have been to hand in some places, only what was memorized and perhaps some written fragments of gospel truths preached by the apostles and their companions were available to the scattered churches. The wonder is that, in spite of all deficiencies, hardships and opposition, the churches thrived and the good news was taken to a lost world with huge success. These people believed the Great Commission was addressed to them as much as it had been to the apostles and they took heed to obey it in all its parts.

The world ever since has never been really different; where Christianity has not reached and prevailed, there heathenism in various forms holds sway. Where fallen man does not know the living God he will have a dead god of one kind or other, a god that rubber-stamps all that he desires and does. The true church is intended to penetrate that world to preach the gospel and make disciples of all who believe. This is the work given to it by Christ and the great periods in its two millennia of history have been those when this work was its chief bent and burden. It must be so still, and not only in Third World regions but in the Western world, which is fast reverting to a paganism which in its human fancies and ways is as grossly superstitious and ignorant as any Third World society.

Obeying 'all things that I have commanded you'

It should go without saying that obedience to the commission requires obedience to its specific instructions — that is, the command is to preach, teach, baptize and make disciples, and the gospel is to be pre-eminent in what is preached and taught, together with 'all things that I have commanded you'. But the fact is that in a kind of general obedience to the commission the specifics are too often curtailed and in some connections, virtually ignored. Were the New Testament not available to us, such departures would not be surprising, but the Gospels, Acts and epistles provide clear and convincing instructions and examples of what the church is to say and do. Yet these instructions are not always obeyed and the examples are not always heeded, and the result is ambiguity, if not something worse, in both 'home' situations and in mission-fields.

Some of the issues arising from this point are considered elsewhere in this book: our concern here is to emphasize that in the New Testament fulfilling the commission in principle did not mean one thing in Jerusalem and another in, say, Rome. Allowances were certainly made for secondary matters like culture and conditions, but it was the very same gospel in every place, with nothing edited in or out; and necessarily so, since there is nothing, literally nothing, that is either superfluous or lacking in the gospel for any people or any place. The whole gospel and its salvation are needed for every single individual, male or female, the Western graduate or the lowly jungle-dweller, 'for all have sinned and fall short of the glory of God' (Rom. 3:23). And though the approach to the jungle-dweller may be vastly different from that to the sophisticated Western graduate, yet in one way or another, the same gospel will have to be preached and taught to, and believed by, both if they are to be saved.

The strange thing is, however, that some churches in Britain are content to support a missionary work overseas which they would not tolerate among themselves at home. One has known instances of friends who are committed to Bible truth and practice supporting missionary work abroad which is not wholly committed to either, or which has adopted views and ways which they themselves reject. The question whether a gospel work in a primitive foreign field can be really different from what it is in Western localities needs to be reconsidered. Essentials laid down once for all by the one to whom 'all authority has been given ... in heaven and on earth' can be neither slimmed down nor stretched out to suit localized situations or individuals; they are for the whole world and for all nations.

If the person who preaches and teaches the gospel in the home church is a man called by God and set apart by the churches themselves, it should be the same in foreign fields. Thus a missionary should also be a man called by God and set apart by a church, and in principle he will be doing in some strange and unfamiliar location what the preacher/pastor does in the 'home' surroundings. In short, the missionary is a preacher and teacher of the gospel; his qualifications are the same as those of the ministers in home churches. The qualifications of elders and deacons in Timothy and Titus were given in a missionary situation; they are for the Christian church and its work in every location and for all time.

The implications of this principle must surely be brought to bear on the modern missionary scenes in which the term 'missionaries' is applied to almost everyone who does something in Christian work in distant lands. It is certainly not my intention to denigrate such people or their efforts, for I readily believe that what they do is a valuable contribution to Christian life and testimony in the world, yet it is still true that so far as they can, all Christians should do the same as witnesses wherever God in his providence has placed them. The same can be said of women in missionary work: their service will always be of inestimable value, especially in pioneer situations where no local help is available to the preaching missionary, but they cannot be preachers themselves in those situations any more than they could be in the pulpits of the churches at home. While we must beware of censuring women who have laboured with evident blessing in various parts of the world, we cannot allow them and their success to be our guiding light. God's Word must ever control and direct us in his work; if he be pleased sovereignly to bestow blessing in exceptional ways we should all praise him for it, but refrain from making the exception our rule.

Obeying the Great Commission is in truth part of that duty which devolves on the church and all its members to maintain the faith in a fallen world. So much of what our Lord taught and demonstrated and some part at least of almost all the epistles was concerned with this serious and difficult responsibility. We do not have to look far for the reason: the faith, like the Lord himself, is under the constant attack of Satan, which means that the church and every believing member are obvious targets for him. The attacks are never frontal; rather they are subversive and subtle attempts to corrupt the truth and to divert God's people in the world into ways and works which in fact are blind alleys of compromise and confusion.

The evidence for this is all around us, ranging from hyper-Calvinism, through reconstructionism and theistic evolution to the 'Toronto Blessing', with many lesser human fancies protruding in between them. These things are all the more insidious because, in diverse degrees, those who promulgate them hold to some essential Christian doctrines. The resulting damage is worldwide — in local churches, both in the West and in the Third World, in multiplying house-groups and in some missionary societies which, not surprisingly perhaps, seek to embrace views and practices which really are at variance with each other. The same society can thus have members in one place advocating and practising their preferred standpoint, and others, at no great distance, pressing contrary opinions. Churches at home too are sometimes unaware that missionaries they have sent out and are supporting to serve in such societies may be obliged to serve alongside others whose beliefs and methods would not be acceptable in their own fellowship.

There is no doubt that all this is hurtful to the cause of the gospel and I take no pleasure in referring to it. It is my firm conviction that the reformed faith is biblical and that all who hold it should not divide on secondary issues which do not impinge upon basic doctrines and experience. Where there is division, separation is better than confusion and contradiction, which leaves many believers in spiritual bewilderment, if not something worse, and the onlooking world in self-justifying complacency. Let Christians everywhere ensure that their own lives and actions combine with others to obey the Great Commission, fulfilling its every clause — that is, 'all things that I have commanded you'.

Jesus came to Galilee, preaching the gospel of the kingdom of God (Mark 1:14).

Preach the gospel to every creature (Mark 16:15).

God chose among us, that by my mouth the Gentiles should hear the word of the gospel and believe (Acts 15:7).

In him you also trusted, after you heard the word of truth, the gospel of your salvation (Eph. 1:13).

And he commanded us to preach to the people, and to testify that it is he who was ordained by God to be Judge of the living and the dead (Acts 10:42).

'... for which I was appointed a preacher and an apostle ... a teacher of the Gentiles in faith and truth' (1 Tim. 2:7).

5.
'Preach the gospel...'

Nothing is more distinctive in the Great Commission than what Christ actually sent his apostles to do in the world. They were to 'preach the gospel'. The various relevant statements in the four New Testament Gospels and in Acts differ in language and emphasis, but they complement each other to provide what in modern parlance could be said to be the apostles' job description. Our modern world has become meticulous in this respect, with laws and regulations promulgated to define duties and delimit responsibilities, for the guidance and protection of all concerned.

In the commission the Lord Jesus, exercising the authority committed to him, laid down once and for all his job description for the apostles: preaching the gospel was to be their chief work, to which they were to devote all they had in gifts, energy and time. They could not have been entirely ignorant of what this meant, for they had seen the Lord himself doing the very same thing since day one of their relationship with him. Throughout that time they must have been impressed as much by the message as by the preaching of it. Though the cross and resurrection were still to come, the gospel Christ preached had in it all the elements of grace and mercy, for these qualities were embodied in himself. In his native Nazareth he had quoted Isaiah's prophecy and said he had been anointed 'to preach the gospel to the poor ... heal the broken-hearted, to preach deliverance to the captives and recovery of sight to the blind, to set at liberty those who are oppressed, to preach the acceptable year of the Lord' (Luke 4:18-19). In essence, this was the gospel of grace which, with a greater understanding following the resurrection and the power bestowed on them at Pentecost, the apostles were commanded to preach, and this they did to their dying day.

This is also the task that all who follow the apostles in faith and practice are required to carry out: their supreme business in the world is, and must ever remain, the same gospel and the same preaching, with every other interest and activity subservient to both. No amount of effort or sacrifice in any other respect can compensate for any weakness or failure in obeying the Lord's ultimate charge to his people. That there is weakness and failure none familiar with the current state of Christianity can possibly doubt. It is no exaggeration to say that almost anything but preaching the gospel has become the vogue in wide sections of Christendom, including professing evangelicalism. The main reason is that the gospel itself has been lost in the mists and maze of human opinions. The word 'gospel' itself has come to mean different things to different people, all of them having no discernible relation to the sovereign grace of God and the unique atoning work of Christ.

We cannot enter here into a comprehensive treatment of the New Testament gospel in all its implications but some aspects must be noted because of their bearing on the Great Commission and on its fulfilment.

The gospel of God

First and foremost is the fact that it is the gospel of God; the one true God is its sole Author and Architect. It is his one and unique means of saving 'a great multitude which no one could number, of all nations, tribes, peoples, and tongues' and bringing them to everlasting glory. The crux of the matter is that God sent his Son into the world to take the sin of this innumerable multitude upon himself and suffer its punishment in his own person on Calvary's cross, thereby infallibly securing their eternal redemption.

It was this truth, this message, this gospel, that Christ entrusted to the apostles. With the enabling power of the Holy Spirit, they were to proclaim it to all the world, and ten days later Peter was doing just that to the large crowd gathered in Jerusalem for the feast of Pentecost. With economy of words he traced the divine origin and historical preparation for this gospel, culminating in the life, death and resurrection of Jesus of Nazareth, all of which had been for 'the remission of sins'. Despite violent opposition, Peter and his fellow apostles persisted in preaching this gospel and, under the Holy Spirit's inspiration, committed it to writing so that all the world might know that 'Christ also suffered once for sins, the just for the unjust, that he might bring us to God' (1 Peter 3:18).

The apostle Paul's gospel was not a whit different. Having been the outstanding practitioner of external religion of his generation, he was brought to know the one in whom, as he later wrote, 'we have redemption through his blood, the forgiveness of sins' (Col. 1:14). Many other passages from the epistles of Paul and, indeed, all the New Testament writers, are unambiguous and wholly convincing that the gospel which Christ charged his apostles to preach is supremely concerned with divine salvation from sin and its consequences, leaving nothing for men and women to do except to repent and believe, and even this is the result of the Spirit's work in the heart.

It is with this gospel that the true Christian church must ever be occupied if it is to fulfil its great and unrivalled mission in the world. There is no other message like it, and there never will be. Jesus Christ and his salvation is God's last word to a fallen world; by this message all who believe can, and will, be eternally saved, but by this too 'He will judge the world in righteousness by the man whom he has ordained. He has given assurance of this to all by raising him from the dead' (Acts 17:31). Nothing can be allowed to deface, still less replace, this gospel; there must be no dilution of it and there can be no substitute for it. 'Let God be true but every man a liar' (Rom. 3:4). If this gospel is tinkered with in any way, Christianity itself is lost to mankind.

What is needed above every other interest among profess-ing Christians in these late twentieth-century days of double-speak and looking both ways is to recover that high view of the Christian gospel which is so characteristic of the New Testa-ment. In his letter to the Philippians, the great apostle Paul epitomizes that view so conclusively. While he anathematized those who were troubling the Galatian believers, he could rejoice in his imprisonment in Rome that some were 'bold to speak the word', even though it was 'from envy and strife ... supposing to add affliction to my chains' (Phil. 1:14-16). The crucial factor was the gospel, which was being perverted among the Galatians but was being preached in Rome, even though the motives of some were dubious: 'Whether in pre-tence or in truth, Christ is preached; and in this I rejoice, yes, and will rejoice' (Phil. 1:18).

For the furtherance of that gospel Paul accepted that 'My chains are in Christ', and that he was 'appointed for the defence of the gospel'. Accordingly he exhorts the Philippian believers to be 'with one mind striving together for the faith of the gospel' (Phil. 1:13,17,27).

Restoring the biblical order

This high view of Christ's gospel, which has also been a char-acteristic of times of prosperity for the church, has become

somewhat jaded among many professing Christians today —
where, indeed, it has not been almost entirely forsaken. The
particular and free nature of salvation has largely given way to
a belief in universal salvation or other kindred heresies, such
as a second chance, annihilation or salvation by works.

What may be called popular Christianity, in Britain and
elsewhere, is wholly devoted to a salvation which is social and
temporal, it being assumed that there is no hell and all will
finally be found in heaven anyway. What remains therefore for
the church and its members to do is to work for the relief of the
world's millions who are suffering in famine, disease or
deprivation of one kind or another. With the vivid and
unflagging help of the media, this 'liberation theology' has
become the preoccupation of established Christendom and not
a few evangelicals have been roped into the enterprise. There
are some Christian missions that have been redirected to
caring for bodily needs rather than for those of the soul. It is as
if the Great Commission has been modified for this time, with
the gospel of eternal salvation for lost sinners changed to a
gospel of liberation for oppressed and famine-stricken multitudes who in any case will not be eternally lost.

Christ's gospel has, of course, always had its social ramifications, as the New Testament clearly demonstrates. Christ
himself healed the sick and fed the hungry, and moreover did
not mince his words in showing his people who the neighbour
they are required to love really is. The first days of the
Christian era also show how the early Christians had a true
practical regard for the needy among them. They 'had all
things in common', not by apostolic edict, but spontaneously,
as those who had much readily shared with those having little
or none, and did so because of the effectual grace of God in
their hearts (Acts 2:44-45). It was the same later with the
believers at Antioch who, hearing of the famine in Judea, 'each
according to his ability, determined to send relief to the

brethren dwelling in Judea' (Acts 11:29). Still later, Paul warmly commended the Macedonian Christians who, though in 'deep poverty' themselves, sent gifts to help others in greater need. Describing their liberality as 'the grace of God bestowed on the churches of Macedonia', Paul exhorted the believers in Corinth to 'abound in this grace also' (2 Cor. 8:1-7).

The clear pattern here is not liberation theology having the pre-eminence, with the salvation of lost sinners taken for granted. It is rather the exact reverse, with the gospel being preached and believed, resulting in the salvation of many souls, and those who have been saved subsequently going on to care for those in physical distress among and around them. So strongly is this pattern emphasized by the epistle of James that where the social concern is wanting, a person's profession of faith and experience of salvation are said to be false (James 2:15-17).

It is this New Testament perception and practice which must characterize the people of God no less in our time than in apostolic days. If most of the social relief in Acts and in the epistles is directed towards fellow-believers who are in need, that only highlights where our first responsibilities lie. But though suffering Christians are first in order, they are not our sole concern, for we are told, 'As we have opportunity, let us do good to all, especially to those who are of the household of faith' (Gal. 6:10). And we note again who our neighbour is according to the Lord Jesus in the parable of the Good Samaritan.

Evangelical Christians should not find it difficult to distinguish between, on the one hand, the glorious gospel of saving grace and its merciful implications in this afflicted world and, on the other, that spurious social gospel so acceptable to a fallen humanity which is ever ready to try to save itself by its own works of kindness and charity. Certainly, none more than those in whose hearts the love of God is shed abroad should respond to those graphic reports of starving children. But those hearts, moved with pity for famished bodies, should not be less moved for the souls of countless millions who have no knowledge of God and are without hope for this world and the world to come. He who is Lord of heaven and earth was more aware of, and concerned for, the deprived multitudes of all ages than his followers can ever be, and he it was who sent his people, not to become social workers among those multitudes, but to preach the gospel to them, make disciples of them and be witnesses to them of Christ and his salvation, so that though they may suffer grievously in this world, they shall be saved for eternity.

The twelve apostles well understood what they had been told to do and they refused to be deflected from it by the growing physical needs of many among their followers: 'It is not desirable that we should leave the word of God and serve tables. Therefore, brethren, seek out from among you seven ... whom we may appoint over this business; but we will give ourselves continually to prayer and to the ministry of the word' (Acts 6:2-4). From that day to this it has never been desirable for prayer and the ministry of the Word to be demoted for any reason whatsoever — not for pressing social demands, nor for the trendy developments of this or any other time. Paul charged Timothy, who was then faced with the many problems and claims of the church in Ephesus: 'Preach the word! Be ready in season and out of season. Convince, rebuke, exhort, with all longsuffering and teaching' (2 Tim. 4:2).

As it was with the apostolic founders of the faith, so it must be with all who succeed them in truth and practice. Serving tables in any sense must not be allowed to take first place in the perception and activity of the true church. The spiritual plight of fallen mankind in the light of eternity, of final judgement and of heaven and hell must precede, though not preclude, all other considerations, however pressing they may be. Powerful organizations, including many national governments with vast resources, are commendably promoting and providing massive relief throughout the world and many Christians are rightly helping them in the task. But the only people who labour to save immortal souls are those who are truly saved themselves and belong to the one and only church of Jesus Christ. Comparatively, they, like those first Christians at Pentecost, are few and frail in numbers and resources, but 'The weapons of our warfare are not carnal but mighty in God for pulling down strongholds' (2 Cor. 10:4). Foremost among those weapons are preaching, witnessing, making disciples and praying, and central to them all is the glorious gospel of the blessed God. Without this gospel there is no true knowledge of God, no knowledge or experience of his love and mercy, no forgiveness of sins, no message of hope for fallen mankind.

Let therefore all who believe and have been saved through this gospel commit themselves to obeying the Great Commission and to praying that it will be preached and taught, as of old, 'by the Holy Spirit sent from heaven'. The one who charges us with the work is himself our best example. He did heal the sick and feed the hungry, but he came pre-eminently to die on the cross for the sins of all who believe in his name. None surely can suggest that his preliminary ministry among the suffering multitudes takes precedence over the shedding of his blood, neither in principle nor in practice. His work on the cross is the good news and is of everlasting significance. It will save all who come to him right up to the end of time and will be the subject of the redeemed in heaven. It must always be their theme here on earth, too.

> The cross he bore is life and health
> Though shame and death to him:
> His people's hope, his people's wealth
> Their everlasting theme
>
> (James Kelly).

Who is called to preach?

While the Great Commission is the supreme business of the Christian church in every generation, and the chief activity prescribed is to preach the gospel, it does not follow that every member of the church is commissioned to preach. On the contrary, while every Christian believer should be a witness to the saving power and grace of God in the gospel of Christ, only those who are specifically called of God are to preach — that is, to proclaim the gospel in an authoritative capacity as an appointed herald, separated and endowed for the work.

A number of aspects of the call to preach will be dealt with in a later chapter, but at the risk of repetition we must give careful consideration to this call, seeing it is such an important matter, and the term 'call' is, alas!, bandied about these days often without really being understood — where indeed its existence is recognized at all.

We have only to look at the men to whom the Great Commission was first given to see that they had already been called to preach. There were clearly many disciples, including several prominent women, that followed Jesus throughout his public ministry, but the commission was only to 'the eleven' (Mark 16:14) — that is, to the twelve disciples minus Judas Iscariot. The Gospels show Jesus going out of his way to call these men who were to be the future preachers. He walked by the Sea of Galilee and 'saw two brothers ... casting a net into the sea; for they were fishermen. And he said to them, "Follow me, and I will make you fishers of men"' (Matt. 4:18-19). It has become too easy to take this and other similar statements and apply them to Christians generally, and inevitably when this happens the application is partial and general. This was a divine call and its implication was surely far-reaching. Those called 'immediately left their nets and followed him' (Matt. 4:20). This is a consequence which invariably accompanies every such call. Hence to apply the text to every believer is simply wrong, making it unrealistic and therefore meaningless.

'Follow me,' meant precisely that for those fishermen, as did, 'I will make you fishers of men.' By the time the commission was given to them they had been called, they had followed Jesus and had been made 'fishers of men'. They were taught the gospel and it was committed to them as a solemn trust which henceforth they would keep and discharge at whatever cost. In the words of Paul in 1 Corinthians 9:16, 'Necessity is laid upon me; yes, woe is me if I do not preach the gospel!' Paul was not among the eleven who were first commissioned, but it was his claim that he was in no sense inferior to the eleven, either as an apostle or as a preacher to whom the gospel had been entrusted. Writing to the Romans he told them that he had been 'separated to the gospel of God' (Rom. 1:1). To the Galatians he said similarly that he had been set apart from his mother's womb, which surely is a reference to eternal election, and had been 'called ... through his grace, to reveal his Son in me, that I might preach him among the Gentiles' (Gal. 1:15-16), which I take to mean that, having been elected, Paul was duly called and entrusted with the gospel of Christ that he might pre-eminently preach it to the Gentile world.

Few things are clearer or more significant in sacred history than that God has always chosen and called men to serve him. Thus it was with Abraham, Joseph, Moses, Joshua, David, Gideon, Elijah, Isaiah, Amos and many more.

And you, child, will be called the prophet of the Highest;
For you will go before the face of the Lord
to prepare his ways,
To give knowledge of salvation to his people
By the remission of their sins
(Luke 1:76-77).

This Jesus God has raised up, of which we are all witnesses
(Acts 2:32).

Therefore, having obtained help from God, to this day I
stand, witnessing both to small and great (Acts 26:22).

I have appeared to you for this purpose, to make you a
minister and a witness both of the things which you have
seen and of the things which I will yet reveal to you
(Acts 26:16).

6.
'You shall be witnesses to me...'

Nothing is clearer in the Great Commission than that Christ gave his apostles a momentous work to do and a specific way in which to do it: 'Preach the gospel'; 'Make disciples'; '... teaching them'; 'repentance and remission of sins should be preached'; 'As the Father has sent me, I also send you'; 'You shall be witnesses to me.' These statements, made at different times and places during the brief period between the resurrection and the ascension, left the apostles in no doubt regarding the message entrusted to them and what they were to do with it. They would also have understood in some measure what this would entail, for they had seen Jesus doing the very same work throughout the time they were with him. He had preached to all and sundry and had taught the people wherever they had stayed to listen. Whereas forms and customs had meant little to him, the sight of ignorant and lost multitudes had deeply moved him to preach the gospel to them. When the Samaritans came out to see who had changed the woman at the well, he could not pause to eat the food his disciples had prepared. 'My food is to do the will of him who sent me,' he said, and proceeded to preach the gospel to the Samaritans, who were soon testifying, 'We have heard for ourselves and know that this is indeed the Christ, the Saviour of the world' (John 4:34,42).

Christ, our example

Jesus Christ was the supreme, heaven-sent preacher and teacher who is the model for all who would communicate the gospel. He preached to thousands in desert places and to small groups in local synagogues where the people 'marvelled at the gracious words which proceeded out of his mouth'. He also journeyed to the borders of Tyre to save one Gentile woman and her child. He continued this work of preaching and teaching right up to his last days in Jerusalem and could say at his arrest, 'I sat daily with you, teaching in the temple' (Matt. 26:55; cf. John 18:20), for this was the appointed way for the message of divine salvation to be communicated — namely through preaching, teaching and witnessing.

What he was laying down for the apostles therefore was nothing less — and it could not possibly be more — than to do precisely what they had seen him doing the whole time they had been with him. There had indeed been occasions when some were brought to believe through miracles; the Gadarene demoniac is one conspicuous example. But the chief purpose of miracles had been to prove his true identity as the Messiah, the Son of God. He cited those miracles to the emissaries from John the Baptist as evidence that he was the 'Coming One' (Matt. 11:3-6). Later, in the upper room in Jerusalem, he chided Philip because he had been with the Lord so long, 'and yet you have not known me,' and went on to tell him, '... believe me for the sake of the works themselves' (John 14:9,11).

As much as the miracles were intended to manifest his deity, they also exposed the wilful sin of those who saw them and yet did not believe in him. Though deeply saddened by their blind unbelief, Christ was neither surprised nor disillusioned. He roundly denounced Chorazin, Bethsaida and Capernaum because the miracles he had performed among them had uncovered their sinful state which, he said, was worse than that of pagan Tyre and Sidon and even of Sodom (Matt. 11:21-24).

Nor, as we saw earlier, had he been deceived by those who 'believed in his name when they saw the miracles which he did... Jesus did not commit himself to them, because he knew all men' (John 2:23-24). He well knew that they were merely impressed with the signs, but were still blind to the truth that they signified. The fact is that if Jesus had been performing miracles solely to awaken faith in those who saw them he would have been dismayed with the results. But his great ministry was not a hit-or-miss affair: he was the eternal Son of God made flesh and his miracles had a hundred per cent success rate which demonstrated and confirmed this fact. He knew the hearts of all men and could say at the end of his public ministry, 'Those whom you gave me I have kept; and none of them is lost except the son of perdition' (John 17:12). Christ's work was entirely free from fault or failure; what the Father had given him to do was done and he could say, 'I have finished the work which you have given me to do' (John 17:4). An essential and prominent element in that work was his preaching and teaching wherever the opportunity occurred; this had been his normal means of making known the gospel and of bringing those who heeded his word to believe in him and to know his salvation.

Thus in commissioning the apostles Jesus was telling them to go and do no more and no less than what they had so often been privileged to see and hear at first hand. They were to preach and teach the gospel they now knew and understood in its fulness even as he, their Lord, had done. They were not to become part of the religious establishment of the day any more than he, Jesus, had been part of it. The gospel entrusted to them was new wine which could not be put into old wineskins, nor could it become a new patch sewn on an old garment. They were rather to go into all the world and proclaim, announce, witness and teach the good news. These were to be their means of communication and because he was going to the Father and would send the Spirit upon them, their success would, in one sense, be greater than his (John 14:12). As the Spirit directed and enabled them, they performed miracles both as works of mercy and an authentication of their office and their message, but these were always secondary to the main task of preaching and, as the work progressed, the miracles decreased in frequency while the preaching spread with strength and effectiveness. We read of no miracle in Thessalonica or Corinth, but Paul could say that in both places the gospel came in power and in the Holy Spirit, his word — which must mean his preaching and teaching — being received not as the word of man, 'but as it is in truth, the word of God, which also effectively works in you who believe' (1 Thess. 2:13; cf. 1 Cor. 2:4-5; 1 Thess. 1:5).

The means appointed by Christ

This was the means of communicating the gospel that Christ had first used himself and then appointed for his apostles, and as the gospel itself is unchanging in its saving truth and efficacy, so is the appointed means. In the course of history it has been when the same message and the same means have prevailed that Christianity has thrived and, conversely, when either has been neglected, decline has set in. The present parlous state of the church is the inescapable result of the one true gospel being replaced by human inventions and worldly methods taking over from those laid down by Christ. The correlation between the gospel and the method of its proclamation, as commanded by Christ, is unmistakable. When his instructions are rightly obeyed, preaching and teaching become the outgoing of the gospel itself. Listening to Peter and

John the Sanhedrin council 'realized [recognized] that they had been with Jesus' (Acts 4:13). As with Paul, so with Peter; Jesus was evident in the words and the way that both men spoke. So it has been throughout Christian history. What is sometimes referred to as the 'Babylonian captivity of the church' in the Middle Ages was the inevitable outcome of gospel preaching being replaced by a sacramentalism devised by men, with an altar taking the place of the pulpit. Successive generations of church people had no gospel to believe and no Saviour to know or to witness to. Their captivity was ended when men began to believe the gospel and to preach and teach it without sparing themselves. This was the Reformation.

Another captivity has now overtaken large sections of professing Christians, who, though claiming adherence to the gospel of salvation, have largely forsaken preaching and teaching for other methods, principally on the basis that the secular world uses them so successfully. If the sincerity of these people is undoubted, their understanding of, and fidelity, to the Word of God must be questioned. The method Christ laid down for spreading the gospel was not one peculiarly suited to the first century but which could be modified, even abandoned, in later centuries. It was the method for all time, to be obeyed by his people whatever the pursuits of a secular world may be. The modern world's obsession with entertainment is no good reason for trying to spread the gospel through a framework of worldly performers and their various activities. When Paul arrived in Philippi, the centre-piece of the community was the great amphitheatre where Greek plays unfailingly drew and held the multitudes. Yet Paul, having reconnoitred the place for a few days, began his divinely initiated mission among a few women gathered beside a small river, 'and spoke to the women who met there' (Acts 16:13). When synagogues were closed to him he preached in homes, in market-places, on Mars Hill and in prisons — in fact any place where people were found — and the invariable method was to speak, announce and witness to the gospel. The message and the means were in complete harmony.

There is no alternative for those who would obey the Lord in spreading the gospel of Jesus Christ. God has indeed intervened with abnormal means on occasion, but that is within his sovereign right and power. It was the exercise of the same sovereignty that appointed the gospel and the means of communicating it. Let those who cherish that gospel cherish the means also.

The importance of personal witness

Communicating the gospel to a lost world is more than pulpiteering. Christ spoke of witnessing too, and the implications of that are far-reaching, for not all Christians are preachers and teachers, but all are to be witnesses. The apostles were witnesses in that they had known the Lord and had experienced for themselves his grace and mercy in salvation. They could therefore speak of him and of his saving power, not in theory or from hearsay as advocates, but as those who had first-hand knowledge of what they spoke about.

As those apostles preached and witnessed to the Lord and his salvation, others were brought to know him and to enjoy that salvation and they of necessity became witnesses too. While the primary means of apostolic preaching prospered, the witnessing of unknown Christians was also greatly used in those early times. Those scattered from Jerusalem by persecution 'went everywhere preaching the word' (Acts 8:4). This was not preaching in the accepted sense — rather they are said, literally, to have 'evangelized'. Wherever they went after leaving the ministry and fellowship in Jerusalem, they spoke of Jesus and his saving work; this had been the reason why they were scattered, but persecution could not silence them. Thus they witnessed, they evangelized, and to such good effect that the pagan city of Antioch soon saw a Christian church rising in its midst.

It is a sad and serious reflection on the faith we profess that this witnessing is not much in evidence in our day, and the reasons for this are many and grievous. Materialism is one powerful factor among believers in the Western world, much of whose time and energy are taken up with acquiring and maintaining possessions, entertainment for young and old, and several holidays each year. With a full life like this who has the capacity in time and energy for evangelistic witnessing — even if the will is still there?

Is not this one of the chief reasons for the 'crusades' and 'campaigns' syndrome of the twentieth century? I do not want to impugn anyone's good intentions and sincerity, but is mass evangelism, with its vast organization and heavy finance, the biblical way? The believers in Philippi (a community known for its pagan ethos and strong allegiance to the Roman Empire) were said to 'shine as lights in the world, holding fast the word of life,' in the midst of 'a crooked and perverse generation' (Phil. 2:15). Their evangelism was not a light being switched on now and then, but a shining out by their Christian lives and their active witness to the word of life.

In short, this is the witnessing required of all Christian believers, and it must be seen as an essential part of the task of taking the gospel to the world. In a real sense, it should be the inevitable consequence of having become a Christian. Being born again and knowing our sins have been freely forgiven through faith in Christ and his atoning death should make us all like those who could not but 'speak the things we have seen and heard'. It is demanding, to be sure, but it is the pattern clearly seen in the New Testament, as received from the Lord himself, and there is no substitute for it.

Rightly understood, witnessing is not only the responsibility of the believer through everyday living, but a great privilege. What gracious condescension it is that God should call his people to be labourers together with him and to trust them with the gospel and its communication! His plan of salvation is perfect and its accomplishment by Christ is complete. His word is for ever settled in heaven and, his power being as it is, it will not return to him void; all of which means that what he has decreed in eternity will infallibly come to pass. Those whom he has chosen will be saved; not one will be lost. They will all come and take their place in his everlasting kingdom.

For some Christians, such glorious truths have rendered witnessing and all evangelism not only unnecessary but a grievous mistake. Yet the real mistake is to follow logical reasoning rather than biblical teaching and example. God has appointed means to bring his eternal purposes to pass. The Bible in a real sense is the account of the means he has used to fulfil in time what he determined before the creation of the world. Without enlarging further on such a vast truth, we can see that Christ's final commission to his people was, and still is, part of the means. Like a shepherd, he died for his sheep, thereby securing unfailingly their eternal salvation, and then he ordered his followers, who were themselves already saved, to go and seek the other sheep in the world, and the way they were to do so was to preach the gospel, to teach it and to witness. It is his will that the incomparable gospel and its blessings should be carried to the other sheep known to him, not by angels who are mere onlookers, nor by the high and mighty of the world, but by sinners who, having been saved themselves through the gospel, can speak of its mercy and power from experience.

Where Christian believers are in default in this matter, for whatever reason, decline and confusion soon follow. There can be no valid excuse for such failure, nor is there any substitute for it. Christians are to be witnessing Christians; churches are to be the very homes and centres of witness, the Lord reigning among them and his ultimate commission held in high honour among them and obeyed: 'You shall be witnesses to me.'

> Come, let us to the Lord our God
> With contrite hearts return.
> Our Lord is gracious, nor will leave
> The desolate to mourn.

From that time Jesus began to preach and to say, 'Repent, for the kingdom of heaven is at hand' (Matt. 4:17).

Let us go into the next towns, that I may preach there also, because for this purpose I have come forth (Mark 1:38).

And he sat down and taught the multitudes from the boat (Luke 5:3).

It is enough for a disciple that he be like his teacher, and a servant like his master (Matt. 10:25).

And with great power the apostles gave witness to the resurrection of the Lord Jesus (Acts 4:33).

Therefore those who were scattered abroad went everywhere preaching the word (Acts 8:4).

Some of them were men from Cyprus and Cyrene, who, when they had come to Antioch, spoke to the Hellenists, preaching the Lord Jesus (Acts 11:20).

And this gospel of the kingdom will be preached in all the world as a witness to all the nations (Matt. 24:14).

7.
The pattern set by the apostles

While bearing witness to Jesus Christ through the gospel is the essential and permanent work of the Christian church and of all who belong to it, it is evident that Christ appointed the role of preaching to be the spearhead of that work. He called and prepared the apostles for what in the fulfilment of the commission they would most of all be required to do, namely to preach the gospel. The fact that those first preachers were also designated apostles in no way demeaned the place and prominence that preaching would occupy in their subsequent life and ministry. To be sure, their apostleship was a crucial prerequisite for the message they, and all succeeding generations of believers, were to take to all the world, for as apostles they were equipped and authorized to define that message — that is, to say what the gospel is and, equally important, what it is not. It was when the truth of the gospel was at risk that Paul for the most part asserted his apostolic authority. Otherwise it was in preaching that gospel that he generally found satisfaction and joy.

Who was an apostle?

The qualifications of an apostle are plain enough in the New Testament, where the number twelve repeatedly separates the select few who possessed them from those who did not. When Peter presided over the appointment of one 'to take part in this ministry and apostleship from which Judas by transgression fell', he laid down the required qualifications in clear terms: 'Of these men who have accompanied us all the time that the Lord Jesus went in and out among us, beginning from the baptism of John to that day when he was taken up from us, one of these must become a witness with us of his resurrection' (Acts 1:25,21-22).

On a later occasion, in Cornelius' house, Peter spoke of himself and his fellow-apostles as 'witnesses of all things which he did both in the land of the Jews and in Jerusalem', and told how 'God raised [him] up on the third day, and showed him openly, not to all the people, but to witnesses chosen before by God, even to us who ate and drank with him after he arose from the dead' (Acts 10:39-41).

The Twelve, therefore, were men who accompanied Jesus during his public ministry, had received the gospel direct from him and were witnesses of his resurrection. The true church is founded on those twelve apostles and their inspired teaching. They are the 'apostles of the Lamb' whose names are said to be inscribed on the foundations of the walls of the new Jerusalem (Rev. 21:14).

If Paul does not fit neatly into this apostolic frame it is because he was an apostle 'born out of due time' (1 Cor. 15:8). He was, in other words, a divinely appointed exception whose credentials were in no way inferior to those of the twelve. He was 'a chosen vessel of mine to bear my name before the Gentiles' (Acts 9:15) and was granted the essential qualifications of apostleship by divine intervention. He met the risen Lord on the Damascus road, and 'Last of all he was seen by me also' (1 Cor. 15:8) may well refer to a subsequent appearance of the Lord to Paul, the precise details of which were not recorded (2 Cor. 12:2-5). At any rate, when his apostleship was challenged he could claim, 'Am I not an apostle? ... Have I not seen Jesus Christ our Lord?' (1 Cor. 9:1). As for the message he preached, he could tell the Galatians that 'I neither received it from man, nor was I taught it [i.e. by man], but it came through the revelation of Jesus Christ' (Gal. 1:11). This 'dispensation of the grace of God which was given to me' (Eph. 3:2) enabled Paul, in contrast to those in Corinth who claimed to be his equals, to assert that 'I consider that I am not at all inferior to the most eminent apostles' (2 Cor. 11:5).

Nothing in the Christian realm is of greater importance than the gospel, what it is and what it does to all who believe it. It follows therefore that those who alone were entrusted with that gospel must inevitably occupy a unique position in the Christian realm. They had the authority to define that gospel and unequivocally to refute any view and opinion which tainted or corrupted it. Not even an angel from heaven could be allowed to tamper with this gospel; it was the gospel of God and of his Christ which had been once for all committed to chosen men both to be freely preached and to be strictly guarded. Eventually those apostles and their helpers were inspired by God to commit that gospel to writing and, in due time, as the apostles, in one way and another, departed this life, their office and its unique authority came to an end, its all-important function having been accomplished.

A wider use of the word 'apostle'

If other men are referred to as 'apostles' in the New Testament it is evident they did not have the essential qualifications noted above. The explanation may lie in the heightened meaning given by the early church to some common words though these retained their usual meaning in other connections. For example, *ecclesia* was the everyday word for an assembly and is used in this way in the New Testament, in Acts 19:41, where the city clerk in Ephesus is said to have 'dismissed the assembly' — that is, the *ecclesia*, which was in fact the tumultuous gathering in the theatre that was baying for Paul's blood. But in 1 Corinthians 1:2 the company of believers in Corinth are called the *ecclesia* of God, 'who are sanctified in Christ Jesus, called to be saints, with all who in every place call on the name of Jesus Christ our Lord, both theirs and ours'. And in Matthew 16:18 the Lord uses the same word to describe all his redeemed people, a usage adopted in Ephesus 5:25 and elsewhere. Thus we have a word with a secular connotation, and used as such in the Word of God, being invested with a deeper spiritual and theological meaning and also freely used in its enriched form.

The same thing clearly happened with the word *apostolos*. Commonly, it described 'one sent forth' — that is, a messenger sent by one party to another. The New Testament has several examples where *apostolos* appears to be used in this ordinary sense: of Barnabas and Paul in Acts 14:4,14; Andronicus and Junias in Romans 16:7; and of unnamed brethren in 2 Corinthians 8:23, where the word is 'apostles' in the original text but is significantly translated 'messengers' in several versions. It is similarly used in relation to Epaphroditus, who was the Philippians' messenger (apostle) to Paul (Phil. 2:25) and of Paul, Silas and Timothy in 1 Thessalonians 2:6. These passages would all seem to represent the word *apostolos* and its plural used with its everyday connotation and devoid of that enhanced content when referring to the Twelve and to Paul on his own.

Reference to the introductory sentences of some of Paul's epistles provides ample confirmation of the distinction he carefully maintained between the ordinary and special usage of *apostolos*. In 1 Corinthians 1:1 the letter is said to be sent from 'Paul, called to be an apostle ... and Sosthenes our brother'. Similarly in 2 Corinthians 1:1 and Colossians 1:1 we have 'Paul, an apostle ... and Timothy our brother', but in Philippians 1:1 it is: 'Paul and Timothy, servants of Jesus Christ'. This can only mean that as a 'called' apostle, equal in all things with the Twelve, Paul had to be distinguished from Timothy, but as 'servants of Jesus Christ' they could be joined together. Timothy had not seen the risen Christ and the gospel he preached was what he had heard from Paul (2 Tim. 3:14), but in his ministry of the gospel he was a fellow servant with Paul and others.

Following in the steps of the Master

The apostles and their immediate successors had no purpose-built or 'consecrated' premises, no pulpit as their exclusive preserve and none of the customary incidentals which in subsequent times have come to be taken for granted. (We are at present simply noting the existence of these things, not their implications.) They preached and taught where they could, like their Master before them, for whom forms and customs meant very little, while the sight of blind and ignorant multitudes moved him to the depths of his being and caused him to preach to them without ceremony or delay. 'He preached the word to them' in a house in Capernaum and 'taught the multitudes from the boat' beside the Sea of Galilee (Mark 2:2; Luke 5:3). Having spoken to the Samaritan woman, he stayed for two days to preach the Word to other Samaritans who testified, 'We have heard for ourselves and know this is indeed the Christ, the Saviour of the world' (John 4:40,42). Among the many or the few, in synagogues, homes or open places, he spoke, taught and preached the good news, and the common people heard him gladly.

Like Master, like servants. Peter's preaching during Pentecost, probably in an open space outside the house with the
upper room, was just the first step in what became the pattern
soon afterwards. The gospel was preached and taught in
Solomon's Porch, in synagogues and any available and convenient place, including Cornelius' house in Caesarea. Paul in
Philippi began beside a river where a few women gathered for
prayer, continued in Lydia's house and ended up in the jail
where at midnight he and Silas were singing hymns to God.
Having started in the synagogue in Thessalonica, he had to
move to Jason's house; in Athens he was in the market-place
reasoning with Jews and Gentiles and on Mars Hill he
preached the Word to questioning philosophers. He was a long
time in Tyrannus' school in Ephesus and eventually in Rome
he preached to all in a guarded house. Many homes of
believers became the meeting-places of local churches and in
later years of persecution the gospel was preached in isolated
locations, caves and tunnels, all of which meant that the
apostles and their successors really did 'go' as they had been
commanded and their preaching could not be confined, still
less silenced.

The continuing task

It is surely one of the major disasters of Christian history that
the ways and means employed by the Lord and his apostles to
spread the gospel became lost when form and institutionalism
took over. Where simple and convenient meeting-places once
sufficed, ornate buildings sprang up, together with ceremony
and ritual, and these in turn facilitated a man-centred control
which had all to do with power and nothing with the glory of
the gospel. Not surprisingly, what Christ had commanded and

his apostles had done was relegated to the sidelines and in time lost in the mists of human ideas and practices.

With both the gospel and its appointed means of proclamation largely discarded, it is not surprising that man-centred religion should increase, as in the current multi-faith movement. Some political expediencies are no doubt hidden in that movement, for the need to maintain peace in a nation and a world of disparate and competing religions is no small consideration. The queen does not attend multi-faith gatherings in Westminster Abbey merely for pleasure; high matters of political and social interests are surely involved. Yet Christianity cannot be merged with other world religions, no matter what the motives may be. Two cannot walk together except they be agreed, and there can be no agreement between Christianity and other religions because the one is from heaven while the others are of the earth and are earthy.

If Christians are charged with being intolerant, they can only reply that truth cannot be tolerant of untruth. The gospel of God's saving grace in Jesus Christ, his Son, cannot be equated with the self-centred superstitions and efforts of fallen men. The Christian gospel is, and always will be, 'the power of God to salvation for everyone who believes' (Rom. 1:16) and must be communicated as such to people of all nations and tongues. This must ever remain the chief business of the church in the world. The Head of the church commanded it, not only for the first apostles, but for all who followed in their train — the true church in every generation.

It is said that the atom that is split itself splits other atoms, which in turn split more atoms, thus inducing a process of chain reaction which produces energy. In effect, this was the means appointed by Christ before he returned to heaven and which was set in motion on the Day of Pentecost. The gospel was preached and Jews and proselytes from all parts of the

Middle-Eastern world were converted and baptized. These converts themselves became witnesses in that world and the work thus begun has continued all down the centuries in spite of opposition, betrayal and gross deviations, not forgetting all the other devices of Satan and his hosts. Apostles and preachers proclaiming the glad news, lost sinners hearing and believing, then telling others what Christ has done for them and the Lord adding to the church those who are being saved — this is what must be the preoccupation of that church and of all who belong to it 'till all the ransomed church of God be saved to sin no more'.

Then he appointed twelve, that they might be with him and that he might send them out to preach (Mark 3:14).

The harvest truly is plentiful, but the labourers are few. Therefore pray the Lord of the harvest to send out labourers into his harvest (Matt. 9:37-38).

Before you were born I sanctified you; and I ordained you a prophet to the nations (Jer. 1:5).

I was no prophet,
Nor was I a son of a prophet,
But I was a herdsman
And a tender of sycomore fruit.
Then the Lord took me as I followed the flock
And the Lord said to me,
'Go prophesy to my people Israel'
(Amos 7:14 -15).

You did not choose me, but I chose you and appointed you that you should go and bear fruit (John 15:16).

Go, for he is a chosen vessel of mine to bear my name before Gentiles, kings, and the children of Israel (Acts 9:16)

8.
The call

The New Testament shows that the apostles were, on the one hand, sparing in the exercise of their unique apostolic authority but, on the other, free and enthusiastic as preachers of the good news. For them the office of apostle was no ivory tower from which to dole out directives to lesser mortals. Nor did they become a professional élite, aloof and separate from rank-and-file believers. The Acts of the Apostles show Peter and John, and presumably their colleagues also, constantly engaged in preaching and teaching, while Paul was an indefatigable evangelist and missionary whose chief desire was to preach Christ where no one had yet heard of him.

As *apostles* these men belonged to what may be said to be the most select body of men our world has known, or will ever know, a unique company fulfilling an office which died with them and whose function had been completed. But as *preachers* they were the first members of a band of men whose number will continue as long as the age of grace remains.

Heralds of the gospel

Although 'preaching' in our English versions of the Scriptures often has a wide connotation, meaning 'speaking',

'evangelizing' and 'witnessing', it is also often used to trans-
late the word which describes the specific function of a herald
— that is, one called and separated to proclaim the gospel. To
'herald' the good news was the task which the apostles were
commissioned to carry out, and it was that 'heralding' which
spearheaded the spread of the gospel from those earliest days
onwards.

A herald is a man chosen and called by God to the work of
preaching and teaching the gospel. When Peter and Paul and
the others were called to be apostles they were at the same time
called to be preachers and, though the function of apostleship
ceased with them, that of preaching the gospel was obviously
intended in the commission to be a permanent activity, for the
Lord promised to be with those engaged in it until the end of
the age.

The work of a herald is to proclaim news, to publish it
abroad in a plain and understandable way. The news is not of
his choosing and it is not his prerogative to select, modify,
shorten, or extend it in any way. His errand and responsibility
are to broadcast the tidings assigned to him, to do so accurately
and faithfully, and to all within his reach. This is the gospel
preacher; he is appointed by God to proclaim the good news
of salvation in Christ, and to do so without meddling with the
message, or manipulating its impact.

It is God who calls

Just as the first gospel heralds were called by God, so it must
always be; nothing is changed for us, any more than for
previous generations. Christ chose and called the first preachers as he willed — fishermen of Galilee, a tax collector, a
persecutor of the young church, a timid young lad from Lystra
and a medical doctor from Antioch among others. His choice

was sovereign and unfettered, as God's choice has always been throughout history. Abraham was chosen from a pagan background, Moses from the Egyptian palace, David from the sheepfold and Amos from his herds and sycomore fruit. God is sovereign in salvation, and equally so in his choice of preachers of the gospel.

Men have frequently interposed their own wills and choice, often with a genuine desire to swell the numbers of preachers and missionaries in the world, but the results have invariably proved disappointing and sometimes disastrous. Many down the years have thought that the world must be flooded with missionaries and have taken steps to achieve that end. Powerful appeals in missionary meetings, accompanied with pressure of one kind or another, have too often ended in sincere young Christians going to mission-fields believing God has called them, only to realize with much heartache that it was all a mistake. The figures for missionary casualties are appalling in some connections, but are not surprising when zeal outruns knowledge of God and his ways. At one large missionary meeting I attended the appeal for candidates was made with very little response. Several appeals followed, each one more pressing than the last, until all who were prepared to go to foreign fields if the Lord should call them were asked to stand. Some stood but, with such an appeal, the amazing thing was that the vast majority remained seated! The point is, of course, that they should not have been placed in such a position; it was man trying to do God's work for him.

The Christian church as a whole has a responsibility for the gospel in the world and for confirming and sending out those who are called, but it is God who calls, and the church should always 'pray the Lord of the harvest to send out labourers into his harvest' (Matt. 9:38). He calls as he wills and whom he wills; there is no élite class of men that is called and no prescribed method by which the call comes; there is no mould

either into which all those who are called are pressed, other
than the spiritual one of godliness and obedience. The called
servants of God have, therefore, always been a motley band of
men of diverse backgrounds, characters and even appearances. From Abel to John the Baptist and Peter to the present
day, distinctiveness has been writ large on God's choice and
appointment.

Still, there are some unchanging elements in every call of
God, even though they may not be uniformly apparent. By
whatever means the call may come, it is invariably profound
and pressing and, as in the call to salvation, effectual and
irresistible. It is just not possible that the sovereign, omnipo-
tent God should be thwarted by man's rebellious will. The
living God of heaven does not worship at fallen man's feet, nor
can he be a beggar vainly imploring man to be saved or to serve
him. He 'works all things according to the counsel of his will'
(Eph. 1:11). Not that he works imperiously, as a despot or
tyrant; he is the God of all grace and mercy and deals with
recalcitrant men through his Word and Spirit and providence
to bring them to faith and obedience.

The reluctant Moses was patiently led to obey the divine
call, and so was the youthful Jeremiah. Jonah in his folly
absconded but the one who had called him also conscripted a
big fish to rescue the fugitive from his folly and, most
movingly, 'The word of the Lord came to Jonah the second
time' (Jonah 3:1). It came the second time to Simon Peter too
and, like the first time, it was beside the Galilean lake and after
another bounteous catch of fish that Jesus publicly restored
him after his wretched denials, and renewed and reinforced his
call to service. Several goads were used to bring Saul of Tarsus
to his knees and many years later he told the Corinthians that
he could not boast of his preaching the gospel; he was not
doing it merely of his own will, but rather because 'Necessity

is laid upon me; yes, woe is me if I do not preach the gospel!'
(1 Cor. 9:16).

Be the means and circumstances what they may be, it is God
alone who calls men to his service, and when he calls he does
not take 'No' for an answer. Would it not have been well for
the Christian church if this vital fact had prevailed throughout
its history? And is it not a crying need of our time that we all
should recognize that the gospel is to be preached and that it
is God alone who calls men to be preachers?

What constitutes a call?

Theories concerning this call have not been wanting, neither
today nor in the past. There are those who would say that every
Christian is thus called and that only those who have valid
reasons, such as ill-health or domestic responsibilities, are
excused from obedience. It was this view which some years
ago led a prominent missionary society to publish a pamphlet
which claimed that only six per cent of Christians obey the call
to service. Such a view is untenable for many reasons, the chief
being that, in effect, it strips God of his attributes and leaves
him a frustrated Deity. That all Christians are to be witnesses
is beyond question, and it is also true that many are not
witnessing, but we must distinguish between things that are
different.

Others would have us believe that an awareness of the need
is the call, meaning presumably that a realization that humanity at large needs the salvation which is only by faith in Christ
in itself constitutes a call to preach. It is true that a sense of the
need of lost sinners can be a factor in a man's call, but it can
also be a factor in the matter of guidance rather than the call
itself. God calls as and when and whom he wills, and it is a call

supremely to preach the gospel; and for the one who is so called this will be a call for life, because God neither changes his mind nor makes mistakes.

The place and circumstances in which those who are called will exercise their ministry is a matter for God's guidance — whether in a home church or a foreign field — and these may change from time to time during the course of a person's ministry. The vital point is that this call is permanent, while the sphere in which it is exercised can change under God's leading.

Though it is not explicitly stated, the state and need of the Gentile world must surely have been weighing on the minds of those church leaders in Antioch when they met to fast and pray (Acts 13:1-3). They were leaders of the first Gentile church, the implications of which must already have been a matter of some concern, especially for the two preachers Barnabas and Saul. The Spirit's words, 'Separate to me Barnabas and Saul for the work to which I have called them,' seem to confirm this. They had been called before; now they were to be separated, that is, specifically guided to exercise their call in regions new. Their work in Antioch was done; others would now carry it on, while they must follow God's leading to 'all the world'.

It needs to be stressed that the call of God to preach thus is not to be confused with other, what may be described as subsidiary, calls. The two often are confused, especially in the missionary context. Adhering to Bible basics, it must be true that the missionary is a man called by God to preach the gospel and doing so under divine guidance, in one place or another, as Barnabas and Saul were led to do. It has become customary to speak of others who are not preachers being similarly called by God. Without doubt, God has led many of his people to undertake to serve him in gospel work in one capacity or another, often in situations demanding self-denial and sacrifice, and it is no part of my understanding or aim to denigrate such service. To the contrary, there is good historic and current evidence to prove that the labour of such people has been richly blessed for the furtherance of the gospel in many parts of the world. Thank the Lord for them!

Nor is this a plea for two categories of Christians, like clergy and laity, involving the use of titles, special dress or prominent positions — perish the thought! Few things have been more harmful in Christian history than the pursuit of status and the ostentation and overbearing claims that accompany it, what someone has described as 'power without glory'! Neither this nor any other brand of superiority has any place among the followers of the one who said, 'Whoever desires to be first among you, let him be your slave — just as the Son of Man did not come to be served, but to serve, and to give his life a ransom for many' (Matt. 20:27). The true call to preach, though it separates a man to a particular office and work, does not thereby elevate him to a superior class; rightly understood it humbles him under the hand and will of God and fosters a sense of unmerited favour and mercy. He knows what Peter meant when, as a fellow-elder himself, he exhorted elders not to be 'lords over those entrusted to you, but ... examples to the flock' (1 Peter 5:3). He can enter into Paul's feelings when he says, 'Since we have this ministry, as we have received mercy, we do not lose heart' (2 Cor. 4:1).

The role of women

Though it may not suit many nowadays, it must be said that according to the precepts and example of Scripture, only men are called to preach, and no amount of aggressive feminism, or the various types of pressure brought to bear in its support, can change that. The fact that several denominational bodies have now rejected the biblical pattern in this respect is merely further evidence that scriptural authority does not count with them. Since they have cast aside the gospel of salvation by grace through faith, what now passes for preaching among them can obviously be done by anyone. The ordination of women, seen in this context, is really a non-event, having nothing to do with the call and separation to the work of preaching. What the fuss is all about is ordination of women to the priesthood in the so-called apostolical succession through the laying-on of the bishop's hands. Only thus, it is claimed, can a woman be allowed to administer Holy Communion and thereby dispense grace and absolution. The sorry aspect of all this is that it has nothing to do with New Testament Christianity. None of the apostles functioned as priests, because they preached Christ as the one High Priest through whose blood all believers are made kings and priests to God and therefore themselves have the right to enter into the Holy Place with boldness (Heb. 10:19). Believers thus have no possible need for priests, be they male or female, of whatever ordination.

In any case, in Bible terms women are not called to preach. The act of preaching of necessity involves an authority if it is to be meaningful and effective, and Paul in 1 Timothy 2:12 says, 'I do not permit a woman to teach or to have authority over a man.' It may be fashionable to dismiss this as a mere reflection of the social order of the first century and Paul's concern not to run counter to it. But Paul's reasons are creational and spiritual rather than social. Man was created first and Eve afterwards, but Eve fell into transgression and then Adam. Moreover, the woman has her exalted place in the creation order for which she has biological and emotional qualities which make her a 'weaker sex', a fact which manifested itself when she fell to the tempter.

The work of preaching and teaching the gospel must needs be authoritative to be meaningful and effective and the implication of Paul's statement is that it is only to men who are called that the exercise of that authority is given. Not that women are thereby rendered inferior; rather they are different, but still honoured by God in creation and his Word and by all men who are acquainted with it. It was women who washed the Saviour's feet with tears and anointed him for his burial. Women also were the last at the cross and first at the tomb. And the annals of Christian history are replete with the exploits of women in places where some men have failed. If God does not call them to preach, he has other calls for them, to work which they, with a spiritual grasp and appropriate professional qualifications, are eminently qualified to do, both in local church situations and in foreign climes. Together with the preaching and teaching these areas of service all comprise the great enterprise to which the Head of the church commissioned his people so long ago.

Now you shall speak to him and put the words in his mouth.
And I will be with your mouth and with his mouth, and I
will teach you what you shall do (Exod. 4:15).

Then I said, 'I will not make mention of him,
Nor speak any more in his name.'
But his word was in my heart like a burning fire
Shut up in my bones;
I was weary of holding it back,
And I could not
(Jer. 20:9).

And he said to me, 'Son of man, feed your belly, and fill
your stomach with this scroll that I give you.' So I ate it,
and it was in my mouth like honey in sweetness. And he
said to me: 'Son of man, go to the house of Israel and speak
with my words to them' (Ezek. 3:3-4).

According to the glorious gospel of the blessed God which
was committed to my trust (1 Tim. 1:11).

O Timothy! Guard what was committed to your trust
(1 Tim. 6:20).

9.
A solemn trust

One of the most significant ingredients in the call to preach is an awareness of having been solemnly entrusted with the gospel of Christ. The Scriptures abound with examples of this, as God's word came to his servants as a solemn trust which took precedence over all else. The Old Testament prophets graphically described it as 'the burden of the Lord' and the only way they could be unburdened was to convey the word to those for whom it was intended, and to do so without fear or favour. But they were not mere conduits through whom the word merely passed to others: they became so intimately related to the word itself as to forfeit all other identity and interests. Thus the psalmist could say that his heart was 'overflowing with a good theme' and his tongue was 'the pen of a ready writer', as he proclaimed the coming of the one who is 'fairer than the sons of men; grace is poured upon your lips' (Ps. 45:1,2).

So heavy was the burden of the Lord for Jeremiah, and so intimate his affinity with it that, when weighed down with insult and reproach, he resolved not to 'make mention of him, nor speak any more in his name', but he soon found that 'His word was in my heart like a burning fire shut up in my bones; I was weary of holding it back, and I could not' (Jer. 20:9). The message he was to take to others had clearly become part of him and he could not deny either the message or himself. This binding of the message with the messenger could not be more vividly exemplified than in what we read of Ezekiel, who was told to '"Eat this scroll, and go, speak to the house of Israel." ... So I ate it, and it was in my mouth like honey in sweetness' (Ezek. 3:1,3).

It is abundantly clear that this vital principle applied in early New Testament times: 'The word of God came to John the son of Zacharias in the wilderness' (Luke 3:2), and he lost his life through faithfully proclaiming it. After his outrageous death it was said of him that 'John performed no sign, but all the things that John spoke about this man [Jesus] were true' (John 10:41). The gospel Paul preached, and for which he 'suffered the loss of all things', had been 'committed to [his] trust', as much for proclamation as for apostolic custody and definition. He called it 'my gospel' on several occasions.

This sense of trust is a continuing factor in the call of God. That call is a charge to preach the gospel, which itself becomes an awesome trust to which time and talent, in fact life itself, are to be devoted. The preacher, seen and understood in this light, is not the mere advocate of a religion, nor yet a lecturer on objective truth. Nor is he merely a witness of what he has known and experienced for himself (something every genuine Christian should be); there is something more which is crucial to his role as a preacher: God has given to him the word of truth, the gospel, not only for his own benefit, but so that, with all his gifts and energy and his very life, he may become a herald of it to all and sundry.

A high view of the gospel

The divine call to preach and the strong accompanying sense of trust and identification with the gospel will of necessity stimulate a high view of the gospel itself, which in turn will inspire a lively proclamation of it; a man who is not moved to the depths of his soul by the gospel will hardly affect others by his preaching of it. That same high view will also sustain and support the preacher in the times of adversity and rejection which will surely come. Writing to the Philippians, Paul could see his imprisonment in Rome as having 'turned out for the furtherance of the gospel', and he could rejoice that 'Whether in pretence or truth, Christ is preached' (Phil. 1:12,18). Writing once again from prison and awaiting execution, he could urge Timothy 'to share with me in the sufferings for the gospel', and then went on to restate that gospel in the loftiest terms (2 Tim. 1:8-10) because it was that same gospel that was sustaining him in the face of his imminent execution. He was not ashamed of his sufferings as a prisoner, 'For', he said, ' I know whom I have believed and am persuaded that he is able to keep what I have committed to him until that Day'(2 Tim. 1:12). As he was keeping the faith despite chains and tribulations, the faith was in fact keeping him. These and other passages show that Paul's high view of what had been entrusted to him inspired his preaching and strengthened him in his many afflictions.

Many have shared those same sufferings for the gospel and found their chief support in the gospel itself, while others have been able to persevere for long years, faithfully communicating the gospel with little or no visible fruit, their high view of that gospel being their strength and stay. What animated the great missionaries of former years to undertake the most tedious journeys and face the most appalling conditions, sometimes never to return home, was this same high view. C. T. Studd expressed it all: 'If Jesus Christ be God and died for me, no sacrifice can be too great for me to do for him.' Conversely, it is the lack of this high view, and therefore a defective call, which has so often been responsible for failures among ministers and missionaries. Doubtless, there have been other practical difficulties which have brought disillusionment and defeat to many, but that elevated view of the gospel, and of the privilege of being a steward of it and being set apart to preach it, has invariably taken God's servants triumphantly through trials and storms, including martyrdom.

A high view of Scripture

Strangely enough, there are nowadays many who profess a high view of the gospel who nevertheless have no similar view of the entire Bible. The Old Testament particularly is thought to be flawed — in the early chapters of Genesis and the story of Jonah, for example. Their regard for the gospel does not extend to the entire Word of God, but this, they claim, does not hinder them from faithfully preaching and teaching the gospel and the other parts of Scripture which they deem to be true and reliable.

While the sincerity of such people and their zeal for the gospel need not be questioned, it is difficult to see how the unique gospel can be said to be true and trustworthy if its only source, which is the Bible — including the Old Testament — is said to be faulty and unreliable. It is surely true that in the final analysis Bible and gospel stand or fall together. It cannot be denied that the historical and theological roots of the gospel of the New Testament are firmly and manifestly embedded in the Old Testament. However high a view of the gospel a man may therefore hold, if this is not held in tandem with a similar view of Scripture as a whole the end result, sooner or later, will be that his view of the gospel will suffer. The history of Christianity over the past century and a half amply confirms this, with arid rationalism first undermining the inerrancy and authority of Scripture, and ultimately dispensing with the gospel itself — thus demonstrating that losing the infallible Bible duly and inevitably leads to the loss of its great, infallible message.

None can be surprised at this because the gospel of grace is the sum and substance of the entire Word of God and the view we hold of one will ultimately be the view we have of the other also. To be entrusted with the gospel of God in the final analysis means its inerrant fountain-head, the Word of God, being an essential part of that trust, and the communication of one will go hand in hand with the communication of the other. Preaching God's Word and preaching Christ's gospel are finally one and the same thing, for, 'The written and the incarnate Word in all things are the same.'

The gospel inspires evangelism

Holding a high view of the gospel has always inspired evangelistic zeal and action. Peter's sermons at Pentecost and in the following days reflected the highest gospel doctrines and moved him to say, when threatened, 'We cannot but speak the things which we have seen and heard' (Acts 4:20). If ever there was a time for caution and diplomacy on the part of gospel preachers it was that occasion when Peter and John appeared before the Jewish Sanhedrin, who had recently engineered the death of their Lord and were now threatening the gospel itself. The church too was barely out of its birth-pangs and large numbers of new converts needed to be discipled and guided. The real danger was that the life awakened through the gospel they preached would be snuffed out before it was weaned. Besides, the men of the Sanhedrin were leaders of the ancient religion from which the gospel had emerged, and with whose

Scriptures it still retained the closest ties. This surely was the time for diplomacy, for seeking a middle way and a formula which would allow a 'live-and-let-live' situation to develop. All common-sense and practical considerations called for compromise, but the apostles' commission and trust demanded positive action to take the good news to all the world. Being let go, they raised their voices to the Lord in prayer that he would 'grant to your servants that with all boldness they may speak your word' (Acts 4:29).

As for the apostle Paul, who held the gospel in higher esteem than he, or who was more enterprising and resolute in bearing it far and wide at whatever cost to himself? The gospel itself inspired zeal and motivated him to action.

It has always been so in all the great periods of the Christian church. Through preaching and witnessing, God's people have reached out with the only gospel that can and does save sinners. The mighty revivals of Christian history all have this in common, that they generated widespread concern for lost men and women, whether in native scenes or in foreign lands. Some revivals were kindled and fuelled by the powerful evangelistic preaching of men who were raised by God and faced their world as Paul faced Corinth, 'determined not to know anything among you except Jesus Christ and him crucified' (1 Cor. 2:2).

Conversely, the ruinous days for the church have been those when the gospel, so-called, has become 'the power of *men* unto salvation', a largesse conferred on all who toe the ecclesiastical line. Those days have returned in the last decade of the twentieth century with most, if not all, popular 'evangelistic' methods and means combining to reject, and even ridicule, the one gospel of God in favour of man-centred counterfeits.

The challenge for us today

In this situation it is not enough for us merely to hold the Scripture and its heavenly tidings in high regard, vitally important though that is in itself; nor can we be content with just defending it. As it was for the first Christians, so it must be for us — we must be 'striving together for the faith of the gospel' (Phil. 1:27); and this means more than faithfully expounding and teaching the truth to those who believe — it means evangelizing too. Christ came 'to seek and to save that which is lost', and told his apostles to 'Make disciples of all nations.' In the main, the acts of the apostles were evangelism and Timothy was exhorted to 'Preach the word,' and 'Do the work of an evangelist.' Evangelism, then, is not an option either for church, pastor or people; it is rather by divine fiat the supreme interest of the true church and its ministry. 'Evangelize or perish' must always be our motto.

It has become too prevalent among many in the Christian ministry, and in missions too, to excuse themselves from evangelistic preaching and action by feeling and saying that they do not have the gift for it! There are, alas, men in pastorates who preach consistently to the converted and rarely, if ever, have a word for any unbelievers that could be among their auditors. There is no doubt that God does give 'some [to be] evangelists', but neither can there be any doubt that all who are called to preach the gospel should be preaching to sinners as well as to saints.

It may be that the practice, now widely adopted, of preaching through one Bible book after another in a rigid fashion has unintentionally cut the nerve of evangelism. If so, something that can be of real benefit has become a strait-jacket and the sooner we are freed from it the better.

The gospel speaks of God's love for lost souls, of his Son dying to save them, of free grace and pardon by faith; how then can anyone set apart to proclaim it fail to be evangelistic? How can any Christian who cherishes the good tidings not be concerned, one way or another, to share it with those who do not yet know it? Should not the love of Christ which constrained Paul also constrain us today — whether pastors in pulpits, believers in pews or missionaries in distant lands? I for one believe it should, and pray that it will yet do so in ways our modern generations have not yet known. Let all who are called to the ministry of God's Word make evangelistic preaching an essential part of their ministry. Such emphasis in the preaching will challenge and stimulate Christians to evangelistic and missionary endeavour.

Part of the greatness of the outstanding Christian preachers of all time was that they could apply the truth of God to both saints and sinners. Some were, of course, especially gifted, but it is also true that it was the central truths of the gospel of salvation that spurred them on. They loved the Saviour and his saving work; they loved to preach him, to proclaim what he has done and why he did it. Their theology was in their hearts as well as their minds and caused them to pity lost men and women and to declare the riches of free grace to them at every opportunity. In short, they had a passion for souls because of the gospel entrusted to them and although we may not match them in exceptional gifts, we certainly have the same gospel and we should surely have the same passion for ignorant and lost men, women and children.

The preached gospel, whether from pulpits or in the open air, in city centres or scattered locations, must always be the vanguard of evangelism. All other evangelistic activity and the life and witness of every believer should be inspired and instructed by it. It is truly hard to see how a church and its people can rise to, and persevere in, evangelistic fervour and work if the pulpit is not leading the way in this. Some men indeed are better teachers of Bible truth than evangelists, while others are better at evangelism than teaching, but if both are called by God they must surely each cultivate what they find difficult as well as pursue what comes more easily to them. In all things let the word of truth, the gospel of our salvation, be proclaimed clearly and without fail for souls to be saved and saints edified. As Spurgeon said to his students, 'Preach Christ crucified; sinners need it and saints love it!'

And he did what was right in the sight of the Lord, and walked in the ways of his father David; he did not turn aside to the right hand or to the left (2 Chron. 34:2).

Teach me, O Lord, the way of your statutes,
And I shall keep it to the end.
Give me understanding, and I shall keep your law;
Indeed, I shall observe it with my whole heart
(Ps.119:33-34).

Then he said to me, 'Do not fear, Daniel, for from the first day that you set your heart to understand, and to humble yourself before your God, your words were heard; and I have come because of your words' (Dan. 10:12).

And all who sat in the council, looking steadfastly at him, saw his face as the face of an angel (Acts 6:15).

But we have renounced the hidden things of shame, not walking in craftiness nor handling the word of God deceitfully, but by manifestation of the truth commending ourselves to every man's conscience in the sight of God (2 Cor. 4:2).

10.
The preacher's life

Essential as preaching and teaching, witnessing and testifying are to the business of communicating the gospel, they are all to be carried out within the context of lives which in themselves embody and therefore express the gospel and its great truths. If the communicating is to be effective there must be no contradiction between the message and the messengers; announcing and commending the new life in Christ requires men and women who are themselves living that life, and are seen to be doing so. In no one is this more critically necessary than in those who have been called and set apart to preach, and are therefore occupying positions of prominence, in whatever circumstances they may exercise their ministry.

Paul's example in Thessalonica

Recalling his first powerful visit to the Thessalonians, Paul could say, '... as you know what kind of men we were among you for your sake' (1 Thess. 1:5), meaning that the gospel which Paul and his partners preached in word and in power and in the Holy Spirit had also been given visual expression in the way they had lived among the people to whom they preached. How vitally important this must have been for the majority of those Thessalonians who 'turned to God from idols'! They were a people brought up in a society shot through with pagan beliefs and practices; it was one thing for them to believe the gospel so convincingly proclaimed to them and to abandon their idols, but what then? What did believing this gospel mean for their daily lives? They had become new men and women, with the life of God in their souls, but what would this mean in daily living? They could not be Christians in faith and pagans in life!

The Thessalonians had no problem, for they had not only heard the gospel; they had also seen it in the lives of those who preached it, and having been converted, they became imitators of those men: 'And you became followers [imitators] of us and of the Lord' (1 Thess. 1:6). The preachers were followers of the Lord, and in following them the converts were following the Lord too. Paul manifestly knew the importance of himself being a follower of the Lord whom he preached, and thus being a pattern of Christlikeness to those who heard him. This meant that his itinerating ministry was not a hit-and-run affair, a quick campaign and then on to the next place. There is in fact good reason to believe that Paul was persuaded to move on from any given situation only when remaining there would imperil himself and his companions or, even more, when his continuing presence would bring trouble to local believers. Otherwise he was in no hurry; he lived among the people, sitting where they sat and adopting their lifestyle as his own. The people saw as much as they heard and there was no conflict between the one and the other. The preached word and the preacher's life combined to declare the gospel of grace with outstanding success.

A striking picture of New Testament evangelism emerges from the account in 1 Thessalonians 1, for the converts themselves became examples to others and made the gospel known 'in every place'. Paul, Silas and Timothy faithfully followed the Lord whom they preached and became examples to all their converts. In turn, the latter 'became examples to all in Macedonia and Achaia who believe' and thereby they 'sounded forth' the word of the Lord. The Thessalonian believers became a sounding-board for the gospel they had received; having been evangelized themselves, they became evangelists to others in no uncertain way, all of which is the New Testament way of spreading the gospel.

Preaching and life cannot be separated

The significance of the preachers' lives in all this is perfectly plain and we must not shrink from stressing it. There have been many hindrances to the effective spread of the gospel, and by no means the least among them has been the sorry failure of Christians generally, and preachers in particular, to practise what they preach. Where preachers have not imitated in their lives the Lord they have preached, debasement of the gospel and church decline have not long been delayed. If preaching and life are separated in the pastor and preacher this will soon be reflected in the people, for as godly living is imitated, so also is ungodly living.

In writing to the Corinthians Paul could claim that 'We give no offence in anything, that our ministry may not be blamed. But in all things we commend ourselves as ministers of God' (2 Cor. 6:3-4). Nothing less than this can be tolerated in all who would proclaim the gospel of Christ. It is no mere coincidence that many of the outstanding preachers of Christian history have been outstanding examples of godly living as well. One critic, writing of George Whitefield after his death, said, 'So simple was his nature that, glory to God and good will to men having filled it, there was room for little more; and inspired with its genial and piteous spirit, so full of heaven reconciled and humanity restored, he himself became a living gospel.' The young preacher of Dundee, Robert Murray M'Cheyne, was famed for his saintliness, and his friend William Burns, so greatly used in revivals before becoming a missionary in China, was once described as 'the holiest man alive'. The ministry of few men, if any, has seen greater blessing than that of Spurgeon and he could tell his wife, 'You can write my life across the skies.' The pre-eminent preacher of our time was Dr Martyn Lloyd-Jones who personally was a very private man. Those who really knew him, however, soon became aware of his God-centredness and his marked abhorrence of self-projection and display. What was true of Paul and his partners in Thessalonica was true also of Dr Lloyd-Jones at Westminster Chapel and, of course, has been true of so many more in the annals of Christianity. Doubtless, gifts and talents have often been prominent in such men, but so too has their godliness of life. Together with their powerful preaching, their own lives were shining lights in the world.

The dangers of materialism

While it is always precarious to generalize, our eyes must not be closed towards trends from which the Christian scene, like society at large, seems never entirely free. When Christianity is not influencing the world it is being influenced by the world, with serious consequences for the church, its message and its people. It is this latter trend which has become all too prevalent in the declining years of the twentieth century, not least among those who claim to be called to the work of gospel ministry both in native domains and in foreign lands. Certain attitudes and practices are increasingly evident which suggest a closer identification with worldly materialism than with New Testament precepts and example. There is increasing evidence that a contract of work and financial matters have assumed greater significance than the preaching of the Word and the cure of souls and, not surprisingly, pulpits and pews are suffering in consequence.

It cannot be mere coincidence that powerful preaching, like general godliness, has declined as material prosperity has increased. Jesus, the master preacher, had no place to lay down his head and the most salient feature of his lifestyle was its simplicity derived from the absence of material things. When he called and sent out his disciples to preach he warned them to be similarly free from encumbering possessions which demand so much time and attention. 'He commanded them to take nothing for the journey ... no bag, no bread, no copper in their money belts' (Mark 6:7). They were to expect their physical needs to be supplied through their ministry. The Acts of the Apostles and the epistles show the apostles living in the same way and exhorting their fellow-workers to do the same. Paul tells Timothy, 'Having food and clothing, with these we shall be content' (1 Tim. 6:8).

The most effective preachers of the gospel in Christian history in the main were poor in all things except godliness and spiritual power. Most, if not all, of the outstanding men of the revivals in the eighteenth and nineteenth centuries lived in comparative poverty, and a few in hardship, and there have been many like them in other periods whose usefulness in the preaching and work of the gospel knew no bounds.

I am far from advocating poverty for its own sake; nor do I condone the failure of churches to maintain their pastors and their families in a reasonable standard of living. My concern is that the prevailing materialistic outlook in the Western world is conditioning some who say they are called to preach, resulting in a preoccupation with things and comforts rather than with the call, the work, the gospel and those who urgently need it. The example of Scripture and of Christian history is in

danger of being lost, and the fear is that the blessing also may
be lost. An Indian rajah said to Christian Frederic Swarz, the
early German missionary to India, 'I have confidence in you
because you are indifferent to money!' What mattered to
Swarz was the gospel for lost Indians; all else was secondary.
It must ever be thus; all who are called to preach the gospel
must be living gospels themselves, examples 'in word, in
conduct, in love, in spirit, in faith, in purity' (1 Tim. 4:12), this
being an essential component in the work of communicating
the gospel to the world. It meant self-denial and sacrifice for
the Chief Shepherd himself and for all who have been like him
in the history of the Christian church, and it cannot mean less
today for any who would claim that God has called them to
take the message of salvation by faith in his Son to a benighted
world.

Preaching the one gospel to people of differing cultures

What this means is that the gospel of Christ is to be not only
preached, but also made relevant to people in the context of
their lives, their culture and circumstances. Much has been
said and written of late about crossing cultures, and even 'contextualizing' the gospel, as if the problems facing missions in
our time were new, or much more difficult than those in earlier
times. Crossing cultures and contextualizing are evidently
different matters, the former being plain in New Testament
times while the latter implies adapting gospel truth to make it
acceptable to certain situations.

In 1 Corinthians 9:19-23 the great apostle shows what
cross-cultural evangelism requires. We can summarize this
passage by saying that, while he did not adapt his message to
anyone, he did adapt himself — becoming a Jew among Jews,
a Gentile among Gentiles, weak among the weak, in fact, 'all

things to all men, that I might by all means save some'. Some
have used the latter phrase to justify way-out methods and
practices, but this is to misinterpret the entire passage, and in
particular the aim Paul had in view, which was 'to save some'.
This means the gospel was not compromised, nor was the
method contradictory; all was harnessed for the work of
saving souls. None can doubt that 'the glorious gospel of the
blessed God which was committed to my trust' (1 Tim. 1:11)
would always be in the forefront of all that Paul communicated
to others in their own cultural setting.

Acts 17 and 18 clearly demonstrate how Paul coped with
different situations, with their respective cultures, while
preaching 'Jesus Christ and him crucified'. In the synagogue
in Thessalonica he opened the Old Testament Scriptures and
reasoned that Jesus was the Messiah whom they foretold and
promised. In Athens, however, his approach among the philosophers was different, beginning with the Creator and his
greatness but ending with the resurrection of Christ and its
implications. In the synagogue in Corinth he solemnly testified that Jesus was the Messiah, having resolved as he ap-
proached the corrupt pagan city to preach the one basic
message come what may. Without doubt the apostolic way
was to adopt whatever was necessary to communicate the
truth, but without conceding anything that would impinge
upon that truth in any degree.

The ultimate triumph of the gospel

One prime lesson must never be forgotten or neglected in all
evangelism, wherever it is undertaken. No amount of human
effort or ingenuity will make the gospel more palatable for
fallen humanity, or easier to understand to those who are
blinded by the god of this world. The biblical message of the

God who is sovereign in salvation, as in every other sphere, has often been diluted in the mistaken belief that it cannot be understood by fallen sinners. The Bible itself has now been reduced to 'simple' English with the fond hope that many more will read and understand it. Some of Spurgeon's sermons published in English and on the Continent were 'doctored' to eliminate Spurgeon's avowed Calvinism which some might find unacceptable. Yet this was the truth taught in New Testament times from Pentecost onwards with such startling results. It is true also that many of the great pioneer missionaries of former years were unashamed Calvinists who believed in election, particular redemption and all the other unique truths of the biblical gospel, being confident, as we should ever be, that God's purpose in this gospel will not fail.

There is literally nothing in the New Testament which allows the faintest possibility of failure for any part of the gospel and its purpose. Some indeed will be told, 'Depart from me' (Matt. 7:23), but 'They will come from the east and the west, from the north and the south, and sit down in the kingdom of God' (Luke 13:29), and the final statements of God to us tell of the defeat of Satan and all his efforts and the triumph of the gospel, culminating in the new Jerusalem coming down out of heaven from God and God himself dwelling among his people (Rev. 21:1-4). The end of the gospel is victory, with Jesus reigning as King of Kings, and it is with this confidence that his people must ever labour with him, taking the divine gospel to the ends of the earth.

Now it shall come to pass, if you diligently obey the voice of the Lord your God, to observe carefully all his commandments which I command you today, that the Lord your God will set you high above all nations of the earth (Deut. 28:1).

So they read distinctly from the book, in the Law of God; and they gave the sense, and helped them to understand the reading (Neh. 8:8).

Make me understand the way of your precepts;
So shall I meditate on your wondrous works
(Ps. 119:27).

I charge you therefore before God and the Lord Jesus Christ, who will judge the living and the dead at his appearing and his kingdom: Preach the word! Be ready in season and out of season. Convince, rebuke, exhort, with all longsuffering and teaching (2 Tim. 4:1-2).

In all things showing yourself to be a pattern of good works; in doctrine showing integrity, reverence, incorruptibility (Titus 2:7).

11.
'Make disciples...'

The five accounts of the events following the resurrection —
one in each Gospel and one in Acts — can all be seen to be
constituent parts of the one all-important commission and
each has a particular emphasis which is vital to its fulfilment.

The force of the account in Mark 16:15-16 is often said to
be the way it encapsulates the commission in concise terms:
'Go into all the world and preach the gospel to every creature.'
The moving account in Luke 24:46-48 focuses on the very
heart of the gospel which is to be preached — Christ, his
sufferings and resurrection, the aim being to produce repentance in the hearers. The contribution of John 20:21, where
Jesus likens his sending of the apostles to the way the Father
has sent him, is as serious and significant for his church in
every generation as it was for those who were first sent. In Acts
1:8 those sent were promised the enduement of power without
which their best efforts, wherever put forth, would prove
futile. The need for that same power has never been greater
than in our own day.

It is Matthew 28:18-20 that provides the fullest statement
of the Great Commission, and one of its main features is the
detailed description of what the apostles were being sent to do.
They were to 'Go ... and make disciples of all the nations,
baptizing them in the name of the Father and of the Son and of

the Holy Spirit, teaching them to observe all things that I have commanded you.' What this meant for them was that they were to do more, much more, than simply proclaim the gospel that people might believe: they were also to make disciples of those believers, to baptize them and to teach them the great truths of the faith and their implications for life and practice. Beginning with evangelism, through preaching and witnessing, they were to continue with the converts, form them into churches and build them up in knowledge and obedience to Christ as Lord and Saviour.

The biblical order

The book of Acts and the epistles are records of the apostles doing just this: converts were baptized and were gathered into churches among which the apostles or their delegates taught the doctrines. Letters of instruction, exhortation and encouragement were written, regular visits made, elders appointed and order established — all of which was in fulfilment of the commission to make disciples of all nations, baptizing and teaching them. The order was conversion, baptism, teaching, and there is no New Testament evidence of any other. But, as with so much else, this biblical order was, for one reason or another — none of them scriptural — changed whenever it suited the views and aims of mere men or their institutions. The net result is that in so many instances conversion, baptism and teaching are now matters of controversy rather than the way of making disciples ordained by Christ himself.

The commission still stands, however, and the business of the church of God remains. Repentance and remission of sins through Christ, his death and his resurrection must be preached to all nations; those who truly believe must be baptized in the name of the triune God — not after being taught but on profession of faith — and they are to be taught afterwards in and through the continuing ministry of God's Word.

'Baptizing them...'

That Christ was not referring to infant baptism in the commission is obvious, and it seems unlikely that either he or any of his apostles are referring to it elsewhere when they speak of baptism, because that would in fact be in conflict with what is laid down in this commission. Nor can one detect any suggestion in the New Testament that the physical circumcision of the Old Testament era was to be replaced by infant baptism. If infant baptism had been appointed to replace circumcision so many of the troubles besetting the early church would not have arisen. The Jerusalem Council of Acts 15, convened to deal with the circumcision question, would surely have laid it down once and for all that children of believers were not to be circumcised as of old, but they were now to be baptized with water. The Galatian churches also would not have been so disturbed by the same issue.

Baptism in the New Testament, as I understand it, is for those who have believed in Christ unto salvation. They have yet to be taught to observe all things commanded by Christ but, like those at Pentecost and in the early chapters of Acts, they have heard and learnt some basic truths about sin and salvation and have believed and trusted the Saviour and are saved. Baptism is the profession of their faith and the confirmation on the part of the church that they are accepted in Christ, that their sins are washed away in him and that they are heirs of eternal life.

'Teaching them to observe all things...'

While I hold to this understanding of baptism, I make haste to
affirm my regard and respect for fellow Christians who
believe and practise otherwise. I admire their faith and life and
would repudiate any hint of a holier-than-thou position and
attitude towards them. I believe that a view of baptism should
not be allowed to bring division among us. The substance is far
more important than the sign; in other words, what precedes
baptism and what follows it are what really matters — namely
the gospel message for sinners to be saved and the subsequent
teaching that saints may be edified. True Christianity stands or
falls with these, as much in our generation as in any other, but
both are now under attack from many directions and in many
ways. The quest for quick conversions has become the all-
consuming activity of some who apparently have few qualms
about trimming and truncating essential gospel truth in order
to achieve their aims. Repentance and faith are blithely and
extravagantly reduced to mere assent and agreement and —
hey presto! — converts are notched up who have little awareness of sin and even less acquaintance with the crucified
Saviour.

What often follows professed conversion is equally dis-
turbing both in home and foreign fields, where short-circuiting
the work required has become so common. The traditional
missionary, settled and living among the evangelized people
to teach and establish them in biblical realities, has been
deemed too slow and too dated: the job can be done more
expeditiously by using modern devices like films and cassettes
etc, coupled with jet-setting preachers and short-term visitors,
playing guitars and singing happy little ditties and repeated
one-line choruses. If this sounds harshly critical I can only say
that many world mission-fields have seen too much of what is
described, not least Eastern Europe since the Iron Curtain

came down. It is amazing what zeal without knowledge backed by adequate finance can produce, especially where 'teaching them to observe all things that I have commanded you' has not been obeyed. This is what the old missionary method was, and still is, concerned with — not only to convert lost sinners, but also to ground them firmly in the doctrines and life which Christ himself initiated, and it is a method which may be too demanding for those whose Christian self-denial and sacrifice are hardly distinguishable from that of kindly non-Christians.

What Christ so firmly ordered his church thus to do has not figured realistically in the great crusades of modern times, which is no doubt one reason why many pastors and church members have not supported them. Actually, these crusades have always been flawed in this vital area as much as in any other. Despite careful organization for counselling and fol-low-up, by the sheer facts of life, time, distance, accessibility, availability and so on, those responsible could not ensure that converts would be taught to observe — that is, to know and obey — all that Christ commanded. The task was beyond them, which is why they sought to link converts with local churches; but how could this prosper when so many of those churches were liberal and modernistic, and believed neither in salvation by faith alone, nor in the great biblical doctrines? Converts were also recommended to Roman Catholic churches, where they would inevitably be taught the doctrines of works, worship of Mary, confession and penance and the mass — not one of which can be remotely traced to what Christ commanded.

The Head of the church had good reason to be concerned that those who were brought to faith in him should be nurtured and fed with the Bread of Life, rather than that they should be left in a kind of limbo to fend for themselves, or to imbibe the concoctions of men which would poison and pervert their newborn belief. He is the Good Shepherd who knows the sheep need pasture and protection and what he commands his servants to teach is intended to provide both, as much among our generation of believers as in the apostolic age. His sheep in every age need to be nourished and made strong for the fight of faith, both within and without.

The fight within, against fallen nature with its frailties and temptations, is not won with round upon round of singing, fun, fellowship and emotional send-ups, nor yet with the kind of teaching which majors on some particular hobby-horse favoured by the leadership — all of which to the young in faith appear so special and superior. Nor will any Christian grow in grace and godliness on an unchanging diet of spiritual milk. Solid food is needed and that food is the word of truth, faithfully read by the Christian and regularly ministered by a reliable and faithful servant of God. It was the pressing need to teach those things Christ had commanded them that constrained the apostles in Acts 6 to arrange for seven men to be appointed to 'serve tables': they had other tables to serve, from which new believers were to be provided with food convenient to their souls, and it was their faithfulness in this task that was used by God to strengthen the first believers so that they were enabled to stand firm in the cauldron of persecution and rejection in which they were soon to find themselves.

Besides those inward corruptions, the Christian also faces pressures from without, from the world of sinful humanity and the devil, with all his guile and devices. The enemy of our souls has no need to attack us while we are still in his kingdom of darkness busily serving him and spreading his cause. It is when we have been translated into the kingdom of God's Son and have begun to obey and follow Jesus that we become prime targets for Satan. Having been born anew, believing the gospel of salvation and therefore belonging to the Lord, the Christian has made a fierce enemy of Satan, who will stop at nothing to deceive and destroy him.

How did the first Christians overcome their own inner failings and resist the opposition and enmity of the world around? It was largely, though not only, through the apostolic teaching. How did Peter help and encourage the 'pilgrims of the Dispersion' whose faith was being tested by fire and who were to suffer for righteousness' sake? He did not tell them to attend emotionally uplifting meetings, nor did he counsel them with psychology — inner healing, self-esteem, and such like — he reminded them first of their election, their 'sanctification of the Spirit, for obedience and sprinkling of the blood of Jesus Christ', and proceeded to emphasize the great doctrines which would ensure that, despite cruel persecution, their faith, love and joy would be 'inexpressible and full of glory' (1 Peter 1:1-8).

In like vein, Paul exhorts the Ephesian Christians, seeing that they 'wrestle against ... spiritual hosts of wickedness in the heavenly places', to put on 'the whole armour of God', which is the great range of Bible truth girding, shielding and bracing the believer's life and experience (Eph. 6:10-18). This was how those early churches withstood and triumphed over violent Jewish reaction, aggressive Roman power and stifling paganism. The glorious Reformation carried the day over popery, its dogmas and powers through this same means — the preaching and teaching of all Christ commanded; and so it must always be: 'You shall know the truth, and the truth shall make you free.'

The need of the hour

At no time since the Reformation has the need for teaching biblical truths been greater than at the end of the twentieth century. With liberalism still riding high, ecumenism becoming a multi-faith movement and Roman Catholicism as arrogant as ever, evangelicalism is diversifying into more and yet more categories. Some claim direct revelations from God and thereby detract from the supremacy of Scripture. Others are content with emotionally rousing meetings in which the ministry of God's Word is no more than an appendage to a time of singing or 'testimonies'. A few are even going so far as to reject selected Bible passages. And all this is happening at a time when heathenism is fast making a return among us. In such a scenario, the crying need of the hour must be for what Christ the Lord commanded to be taught as never before. And what he commanded is to be found in the Bible, and nowhere else.

Two obvious questions arise, the one related to the other and both of fundamental importance in the prevailing situation. How is the teaching to be carried out, and who is to be taught? Books almost without number have appeared, claiming to provide know-how and practical answers to the questions. But methods, sincere even if novel and sometimes brash, have not been matched with lasting success. Our dilemma remains: how do we reach the multitudes to make disciples for Christ?

We must surely begin with a restored confidence in the Head of the church and in his eternal purpose, the outworking and fulfilment of which is the one and only business of the Great Commission. Christ did not send his apostles and their successors on a random mission: 'Known to God from eternity are all his works' (Acts 15:18). This is just as true in relation to the gospel and his church on earth as in any other respect, and no part of them will or can fail. Nor did Christ leave his apostles or their successors to scratch around for means and methods. Both the charge and the pattern are laid down in his Word for all who will pay heed.

But do we, at this late hour, have anything more than lip-service and mental assent for it all? Some, it is to be feared, adopt an almost fatalistic approach to the status quo, while at the other extreme are those whose enthusiasm leaves all else adrift. In between are a number whose confidence is waning and whose efforts are tired. We need a revival of faith in the triumph of Christ and of his cause, in his Word and his saving power, and in the means appointed for us to serve him and to make the number of his disciples complete. We must believe that the preaching of the gospel and the witness of Christians can be as effective as ever for the salvation of souls in our time, and we must teach them the things of Christ without wavering.

But all must be living, vital and free. We must not preach or teach with staleness, nor dole out doctrine and consecutive studies as mere information — impersonal, cold and lifeless. 'The kingdom of God ... is righteousness and peace and joy in the Holy Spirit' (Rom. 14:17). There must be negative teaching where required and all truth must have application to life and experience. As someone has said, 'The truth is not to be applauded; it is to be applied.' But preaching and teaching must be in the riches of the grace and mercy of the gospel and in that God-given spirit 'of power and of love and of a sound mind' (2 Tim. 1:7). In God's goodness with such a ministry the sects, cults and every spurious version of the faith will meet greater resistance than hitherto and the gospel of the grace of God will spread again to the saving and sanctifying of fallen men and women.

And lo, I am with you always, even to the end of the age
(Matt. 28:20).

But you shall receive power, when the Holy Spirit has come
upon you, and you shall be witnesses to me in Jerusalem,
and in all Judea and Samaria, and to the end of the earth
(Acts 1:8).

Do not be afraid, but speak, and do not keep silent; for I am
with you, and no one will attack you to hurt you; for I have
many people in this city (Acts 18:9-10).

Who has made man's mouth? Or who makes him dumb or
deaf, or seeing or blind? Is it not I, the Lord?
Now then go and I, even I, will be with your mouth, and
teach you what you are to say (Exod. 4:11-12, NASB).

'Do not be afraid of their faces, for I am with you to deliver
you,' says the Lord (Jer. 1:8).

12.
'Lo, I am with you always...'

Nothing in the Great Commission is of greater significance than the promise: 'And lo, I am with you always, even to the end of the age.' This promise was clearly not a mere after-thought intended to encourage apostles who were already baulking at so impossible a charge. Linked to what has gone before by the conjunction 'and', it is an integral part of the commission itself, making it at once both realistic and certain of total success. If Matthew alone states the promise in its most explicit and concise form, the other accounts convey the same truth, though with minor differences.

A work that only God can do

What is plain in every account is that the Lord of glory did not send his people to make disciples of the nations of the whole world 'under their own steam', as it were. The work involved, with its spiritual nature and eternal implications, does not fall within the ambit of human ability, however great or sanctified the latter may be. Changing sinners into saints is a work that only divine power can achieve, which is the precise reason for the promise being given. To think it can be accomplished by any human means is to be ignorant of the real nature of the message and its great object in the purpose of God. To attempt its accomplishment without the presence and power of the one whose promise is an essential part of the very mission is nothing short of being engaged in a wild goose chase!

The apostles from Galilee were despatched on an assignment, the like of which had not been known before and has never been known since. These men, who were for the most part uneducated and of lowly status, were to proclaim a message, the heart of which would stand established religion and worldly wisdom on their heads. Enemies of many kinds awaited them — influential Jews who had recently engineered the crucifixion, Gentiles with vested interests in paganism, and in the background a seemingly all-powerful Roman Empire which could at will kill or scatter its foes — real or supposed — without mercy. Behind all of them the prince of this world, by a thousand ways and means, would fight to keep his captives in his deadly thrall.

How was the gospel of 'Jesus Christ and him crucified' to be preached by such men in such a situation? How can that very same gospel be preached to a lost world about to enter the twenty-first century? How were a small and despised group of intruders to establish a new humanity, redeemed through sovereign grace and regenerated by divine power — in short a true church — in a world of gross sin and false religion? And how can it be done today by similarly despised Bible-believing men in the same kind of world? The answer then was in the promise and it is there still: 'And lo, I am with you always, even to the end of the age.'

The fact is that the Great Commission is complete in itself: from start to finish it covers every essential aspect of the work of taking the news of Christ and his salvation to the ends of the earth. No part of that work is overlooked and no measure required for its success is omitted. Jesus had no blind spots in his understanding, no deficiency in his resources and no need for contingency plans in case of fault or failure. The commission thus requires no adjustment or adaptation, neither in message nor method, in the world of the late twentieth century any more than it did in the first or any other century.

Galloping technology has certainly changed man's environment and has greatly affected his culture, but man himself is still what he was when he was cast out of paradise — a fallen creature with no faculty for spiritual reality. He needed then to be born again and he needs it now just as much. This was the reason for the admonition given in the upper room: 'Without me you can do nothing' (John 15:5), and it was the reason for the promise in the commission. 'The natural man', says Paul in 1 Corinthians 2:14, 'does not receive the things of the Spirit of God, for they are foolishness to him; nor can he know them, because they are spiritually discerned.' This is self-evidently how it is still: no one understands; none seeks after God; there is no fear of God in the natural man. Today, as much as at any time in history, the Lord's promise is essential, in its glorious fulfilment, if we are to see any marked advance in our obedience to his command.

What did the Lord mean by the promise?

While comparatively large numbers of Christians are still committed through various activities and prayer to fulfilling the Great Commission, seriously conflicting views of the Lord's promise and its ramifications are all too common among them. For too many it appears the promise has no significance for the actual work of evangelism today. It is seen rather as a benign presence which only provides general approval of any and every effort at communicating the gospel. Jesus apparently is not present with his people as Lord and Master, nor yet as the Giver of wisdom and power for the obedience to his commands. With some it would appear that his way and his presence in themselves are thought to be quite inadequate for the changing scenes and conditions of the technological age and the important thing is that we should be helping him, doing what we think is best. Thus all the latest knowhow and methods of a degenerate world are harnessed to spread the message of salvation in ways which, however unintentionally, suggest in effect that the commission's promise has been reversed from 'I am with you always,' to 'We are with you always,' in order to ensure its success in the modern world.

The assumption that the Saviour is always present with any effort to spread the gospel, or any part of it, is surely not supported by the facts. Any examination of current Christianity in the Western world must conclude that the one thing which is clear above all others is that the Lord is not present with us today in the intended sense of his promise. If we look at some of the other promises he made which would appear to be comprehended in this final promise, some understanding of what he meant may be gained. To the eleven apostles in the upper room a few weeks previously he had said, 'I will not leave you orphans; I will come to you' (John 14:18), meaning certainly that his people were not to be like bereaved and defenceless children, left to their own wits, energy and nimble-footedness to eke out a way of life. The point Jesus was making was that his followers were not to be like that because 'I will come to you', thus ensuring that they were not to live and work by their own will and wits.

After his resurrection Jesus promised that the apostles would be 'endued with power from on high' (Luke 24:49) and before he ascended he once again gave them this pledge: 'You shall receive power when the Holy Spirit has come upon you' (Acts 1:8). These and other promises were all comprehended in the crucial undertaking he gave as he sent the apostles to do his will: 'Lo, I am with you always, even to the end of the age.' The marrow of it all, both for the apostles and for all who follow in their train, is that the Lord is present with them, not to act as a rubber-stamp for any and every effort they might make, but as their guide and the source of their power. That is a truth which has not been grasped, or has been disregarded, by many who may otherwise be eager and sincere. Nothing could be more important than that it should now be recovered and implemented in all gospel work. The realization of this truth would prevent *carte blanche* being automatically claimed for any effort or practice which appears to bring 'results'. In all conscience, the modern obsession with methods to produce instant results does imply that the programme our Lord laid down for the apostles when he gave his promise to be with them has been played out in earlier, less sophisticated generations, and that in order to fulfil the mandate in our 'new age' Christians have to take matters into their own hands, but they can still count on Jesus to be with them, in one sense or other!

A century or so ago, General Booth, who founded the Salvation Army, was asked by some journalists what was the greatest peril in the future. Like a flash he replied, 'The world's greatest and immediate peril is that the church will offer the world a philosophy of Christianity that provides forgiveness without regeneration — a Christianity without Christ, a religion without the Holy Ghost, politics without God and heaven without hell.' Remarkably this summarizes what, very largely, passes for Christianity today — and that not only in liberal circles, but even among many who claim to be evangelicals. Essentially this is what Paul was speaking of when he warned Timothy about the danger of 'having a form of godliness but denying its power' (2 Tim. 3:5). From such people, said the apostle, 'turn away'. Such attitudes and efforts, however sincere, are the antithesis of the true gospel and of what the Saviour intended when he promised to be with those who preach it. In reality this philosophy is a sub-Christian religion, since the living Lord Jesus is missing from both its message and its practice.

The yawning gap which exists between God Almighty and mortal man has meant that man has always found it extremely difficult to conceive of God being present in the world in any sense. The Athenian philosophers were ignorantly worshipping an unknown God but evidently had no concept of his being present in any sense with his worshippers. 'Him I proclaim to you,' said Paul to them, asserting that 'He is not far from each one of us; for in him we live and move and have our being' (Acts 17:23,27-28). Whether humanity believes it or not, its very existence is in, and wholly dependent upon, the immanent presence of its Creator. In this sense the divine presence has never been absent from the created universe. But in promising to be with his chosen people to the end of the age, Jesus was not merely reaffirming the general truth of divine omnipresence; rather he was explicitly undertaking to be present among and with them in an intimate and active way, a way which would be known and enjoyed by his own people, but not by others.

God's special presence with his people

Whatever may have been new in the Saviour's promise and its first fulfilment at Pentecost, God's presence with his chosen people in a personal and familiar way has always been one of the truly distinguishing features of biblical religion, though, to their great loss, they have too frequently failed to live in the security and joy of it. Having been called to Canaan, Abraham was not left to a nomadic life in a generally pervasive divine presence. God 'appeared' to Abraham, communicated with him, told him to 'Walk before me', and called him 'my friend'. Abraham's failure was to think that God was not with him in Egypt or Gerar, and therefore could not protect him and Sarah as his wife. Jacob too thought God was back at home with Isaac his father, whom he had left in Beersheba, but discovered at Bethel that God was there too: 'Behold, I am with you and will keep you wherever you go.' Jacob responded by confessing his ignorance: 'Surely the Lord is in this place, and I did not know it' (Gen. 28:15,16).

The pillar of cloud by day and fire by night was the visible manifestation of God's presence with Israel in the desert, replaced later by the Shekinah glory over the mercy-seat in the Most Holy Place. This was more, much more, than the omnipresence of God, which was as true for Israel as for the dark and idolatrous nations around them: it was the one true God being with his children in protection, guidance and strength. Moreover the Lord who was in the cloud and fire and whose glory was in the temple was the one who became Immanuel — God with us, thereby demonstrating once and for all that he is with his people in grace and power.

Moses clearly saw God's presence as the distinctive attribute of the redeemed. After the outbreak involving the worship of the golden calf, God promised, 'My presence will go with you,' which elicited this profound utterance from Moses: 'How ... will it be known that your people and I have found grace in your sight, except you go with us?' (Exod. 33:14-16). For Moses, and indeed for all time, the hallmark of the true people of God is that he is evidently among and with them, not only as a propositional truth, but as a living and recognizable reality. In the restored Jerusalem, Zechariah prophesied that men of every language would grasp the sleeve of a Jew and say, 'Let us go with you, for we have heard that God is with you' (Zech. 8:23).

This special presence of God with his people was surely embraced in what Jesus was promising the apostles, and it was to become the outstanding factor in their life and ministry. Even their enemies 'realized that they had been with Jesus', because his presence and power were with them. His promise to them had been fulfilled when the Holy Spirit came down at Pentecost and became their source of strength and enabling for the mission entrusted to them.

Pentecost and the fulfilment of the promise

Pentecost, however, has been seen by many Christians as being the once-for-all fulfilment of the Saviour's promise. Since then, they say, it has been the Christian's right and duty to assume that the Lord is with us and to live and work accordingly. One consequence of this understanding of the promise is the belief is that, as the church obeys the commission, the Lord will always be present, whatever the current circumstances may be. Did he not also assure his people, 'I will never leave you nor forsake you'? (Heb. 13:5). On the basis of this assurance very many servants of God have laboured long and hard in churches and gospel missions in foreign fields, and are still doing so throughout the world. One hesitates to voice any criticism of these friends, not only because of their evident godliness and steadfast labours, but also because of the profound element of truth contained in this view. None can deny that at Pentecost the Head of the church came once and for all time to be with his redeemed people. It was the Spirit who led the apostles into all the truth which they, in their turn, were to preach and teach to others, and who inspired them to record that truth for all posterity. It is he who now gives understanding of the truth and who gives life to those who are dead in trespasses and sins, convincing and bringing them to repentance towards God and faith in Jesus Christ. He is the Comforter who ministers the grace and peace of God to believers and, in all this and more besides, the Lord Jesus, through the activity of the Holy Spirit, is keeping the merciful promise which was given so long ago, but which remains as undimmed and unfailing as when it was first made.

The promise of power

Accepting all this to be true, I still believe it is only part of what Jesus meant by his promise and that we cannot rest content with it. Jesus spoke of power being given to the apostles, particularly in relation to the task set out in the commission of taking the gospel to every creature: 'Tarry in the city of Jerusalem until you are endued with power from high' (Luke 24:49); and again, 'You shall receive power when the Holy Spirit has come upon you' (Acts 1:8). Above all, this is what the apostles experienced at Pentecost and afterwards. Certainly this power was manifested to some degree in all the apostles' ministry and has been ever since in the work of the true church. But at Pentecost, and on many occasions since, there was an overwhelming energy from heaven which none could resist or gainsay, and the great concern now is that the twentieth-century church knows little about such an experience.

True, some friends are claiming that tongues-speaking, healings, prophecies, gifts of knowledge, trances, hysterical laughter, animal noises and similar phenomena are the outpourings of power in our time. However, whatever else these goings-on may be, they would not appear to be the enduement of power the Lord promised. We cannot enlarge here on the issues involved, but to my mind the so-called gifts and blessings themselves evince that they are not of the heavenly power. What that power did in New Testament records, and has done repeatedly since, was to bring an irresistible awareness of God which humbled sinners before him in a way rarely known nowadays. It was this power which converted three thousand through the first apostolic message and which soon broke out of Jerusalem to conquer many more thousands of Jews and Gentiles. It has done the same things in revivals far and wide and thus enabled God's people to fulfil the Great Commission among many nations. It is the marked absence of that power, all claims notwithstanding, that has opened the door to all kinds of makeshift contrivances which confuse many, but convert none.

Some would say that George Whitefield was the greatest evangelist ever seen or heard in the English-speaking world. Multitudes were converted wherever he preached from the age of twenty-three onwards. When the noted American preachers of the period, Samuel Davies and Gilbert Tennant, were in London they went on a Sunday morning to hear Whitefield preaching. As they returned to their lodgings afterwards Tennant is reported to have asked Davies what he thought of Whitefield. Davies replied, 'His matter was ordinary but his unction was heavenly!' Unction is just another word for the power the Saviour promised and, without question, this is what is acutely and urgently needed now if we are to see any signal advance in the mission entrusted to us.

And with great power the apostles gave witness to the resurrection of the Lord Jesus. And great grace was upon them all (Acts 4:33).

For our gospel did not come to you in word only, but also in power, and in the Holy Spirit and in much assurance (1 Thess. 1:5).

And my speech and my preaching were not with persuasive words of human wisdom, but in demonstration of the Spirit and of power (1 Cor. 2:4).

For the kingdom of God is not in word but in power (1 Cor. 4:20).

13.
'You shall receive power...'

It is plain that Jesus' promise to be with his people always was spiritual, not physical. It was a promise to be with his church in enabling power, making their efforts to be effective which otherwise would be utterly vain. The regeneration and conversion of a lost sinner requires a power only found in the Godhead. It is a power which awakens the spiritually dead to newness of life and delivers sinners from the power of Satan and translates them into the kingdom of the Son of his love (Col. 1:13).

What is this power?

Two words in the original language, *exousia* and *dunamis*, have been translated as 'power' in older English versions of the Bible, notably the Authorized Version, but they do not have precisely the same meaning. The word *'exousia'* strictly means 'authority' and is rendered thus in later versions of the English Bible. Both words are found in connection with the Great Commission. Matthew's fuller account includes the Lord's amazing preface to it: 'All authority *(exousia)* has been given to me in heaven and on earth' (Matt. 28:18); while Luke gives the promise of power *(dunamis)* in Luke 24:49 and in Acts 1:8.

The AV rendering of *exousia* as 'power' need surprise no one, for real authority necessarily implies power; authority without the power to exercise it is nothing but a sham. The centurion in Luke 7:8 said he was 'placed under authority'; accordingly he had the power to 'say to one, "Go," and he goes, and to another, "Come," and he comes'. When Jesus therefore claimed that 'All authority has been given to me in heaven and on earth,' he was saying that he had the power to tell his followers what they were henceforth to do and how they were to do it. This is what the Great Commission really is: it is not an outline programme for discussion, nor is it a schedule to be modified and changed as subsequent generations might prefer. Divine authority means that one option is offered by the Lord, and that is to obey. As his people obey he has promised to be with them, thus ensuring the ultimate success of their labours.

This word *'dunamis'* is invariably translated 'power' in the New Testament. It means strength, force and the ability to bring to pass what has been intended. When Mary asked the angel Gabriel how she, an unmarried virgin, could bear a child, she was told that 'The Holy Spirit will come upon you, and the power *[dunamis]* of the Highest will overshadow you' (Luke 1:35). 'The Highest' meant God, with whom 'Nothing will be impossible' (Luke 1:37). In Romans 1:16 Paul said, 'The gospel of Christ ... is the power *[dunamis]* of God to salvation,' which means, surely, that God's power is in the gospel and it therefore cannot fail. Many other examples of *dunamis* could be adduced, all bearing the same eloquent meaning of enabling power, which ensures the accomplishment of the purpose for which it is given.

The promise and its implications

There can be no doubt that Christ's promise to be with his people to the end of the age and the two promises in Luke and Acts that they would receive power for their awesome task are in fact one great pledge which was first fulfilled on the Day of Pentecost. The coming of the Holy Spirit in power was none other than the Lord Jesus keeping his word to be with his people to the end of the age. Having been exalted to 'the right hand of the majesty on high', he came by the Spirit, bringing the enduement of power for which he had told them to wait and which would enable them to do what had been commanded. Peter certainly had no illusions about what was happening to him and those with him at Pentecost: 'He poured out this which you now see and hear' (Acts 2:33).

Two truths of profound and permanent significance relate to the promises of Jesus which were fulfilled at that Pentecost. One is that without that fulfilment the grand design of the commission would not have been realized in any measure. If ever a body of men were properly prepared for their life's work it was the apostles. Having been three years with the Lord, witnessing his power in miraculous works and having experienced it in some degree in their own preparatory ministry, they truly had been made ready for what was to be their life's mission. But even they could not by their own efforts make disciples of darkened and lost nations. Freeing the captives of Satan and bringing them to God, to the new birth and faith in a crucified Saviour is, and always will be, a work lying above and beyond the ability of men. It is a work in a realm into which natural man cannot enter in his own strength and in which his most phenomenal talents can have no effect. Only the power of God by his Spirit can regenerate sinners, forgive sin and save lost souls. Any suggestion, pretence or effort otherwise made is doomed to failure. Success in this work depends wholly upon the fulfilment of the Lord's promise.

The other truth is equally profound in its implications. This is that with the promise having been fulfilled at Pentecost and afterwards, the design of the commission cannot fail; it must and will be brought to a glorious consummation. The gospel will be preached; disciples will be made of world nations; vast multitudes will be brought into the kingdom of heaven; the great plan of God will be accomplished. Not even the failure of his people will prevent its final realization, for the power of the Lord who has promised to be with them is a guarantee of ultimate success.

The problem facing the church today

This being so, the question of the twentieth-century church's obvious lack of success has to be faced. Why is it that, in the era of unparalleled ease of communications, real and wide-spread success in the work of saving souls is so sparse and so small? Never has there been a time when the means of conveying the gospel to the world were so many or so far-reaching, even to the remotest ends of the earth. Besides the very many missionaries continuing to serve in countries across the world, we now have radio and television, videos and cassette-players, films and pamphlets, Bibles and books by the million saturating vast populations, and yet the harvest is meagre in most places and in too many is almost non-existent. So many good and godly people have laboured hard and long, but have seen very little fruit in making disciples of lost sinners. Many of the faithful have rightly consoled themselves in the grace of perseverance, concluding, as they should, that the blessing of heaven is not automatic and cannot be taken for granted. They have therefore prayed, and continue to do so, but the heavens remain as brass.

This barrenness has persuaded others that new methods must be adopted and these have been increasingly novel and complex, in general merely imitations of the entertainment and commercial methods of the world. Surprisingly and sadly, large numbers have been caught in the swell of apparent success and there has been much prating about signs and wonders by various leaders. But where is real evidence of that power as it is so often seen in real revival? Despite brash claims, it is to be feared that the signs owe more to human credulity than to divine activity and the wonder is that any should talk about these things in terms of revival. We must ask, where are the signs and wonders seen so often in bygone revivals, with heartfelt conviction of sin, numbers of sinners turning to God in repentance and faith and great interest awakened in the cause of Christ in the world? Technological devices and adopting worldly methods to present a partial gospel message simply have not worked.

The method laid down in the commission and demonstrated in Acts is the one that has worked in the past and that will still work: that is, the Lord being present with his people as they preach and teach the gospel to a lost world. To think and act otherwise is the sin of unbelief, something which has repeatedly plagued professing believers down the ages. The current emphasis on culture is surely part of this ancient unbelief, though it is fashionable to regard it as a latter-day perception. Though it is expressed in a different way, it is the same sin that led early Israel to fraternize with heathen nations and to syncretize the religious beliefs and practices of these peoples with their own God-given faith. It was, at its core, unbelief in the God who had promised to be with them; instead of believing and obeying him they sought consensus with their enemies and suffered for it. The modern church is doing so still by trimming its sails to catch the various cultural winds, rather than believing the word of the Lord and calling upon him to grant us another manifestation of his presence with and among us.

The danger implicit in rejecting the excesses and unbelief around us is a failure to see the mote in our own eyes — in this case, to take the Saviour's promise for granted. Accepting that he came by his Spirit at Pentecost, with all that meant for the launching of the Christian church in the world, we tend to assume that his promise was then fulfilled in its entirety and all that remains for his people is to believe that he is now with them in the full sense intended in his gracious promise. Did he not say 'always' and 'even to the end of the age'? He kept his promise by coming at Pentecost and we must now believe he is present and work in the knowledge of it, whether we are conscious of it or not. Undoubtedly this is true up to a point and we should always be thankful that he will never leave nor forsake his own.

Yet this cannot be all that is meant for more than one reason. His presence at Pentecost was not only something the apostles were assured in their heads was true; they actually felt his power, both in their own spiritual experience and in the enabling given them for, and in, the work which they then began. The fact that the Lord had kept his promise was a vivid reality and the power *(dunamis)* he had spoken of was evident in the fruits which accompanied the preached gospel.

To think that this demonstration of power was intended only for the birth of the church in the world is to call in question what the Lord meant in saying 'always' and 'to the end of the age'. If the commission was for all time, then surely the power given for its accomplishment was equally so; otherwise we have to believe that, having come with divine power to initiate the task he had laid down, Jesus then left the continuation and ultimate completion of it in the hands, and within the capacities, of his followers, with whom he would always be present in some measure. Probably few, if any, Christians would specifically hold and enunciate such a view, but it is what is implied in practice among some groups, even if unintentionally.

This view also calls in question the evidence of Acts and some of the New Testament epistles. The book of Acts records several manifestations of this same power subsequent to Pentecost, and not only in the performance of miracles. Following the healing of the lame man at the gate of the temple in Acts 3, Peter again preached Jesus Christ, repentance and forgiveness of sins to the gathered multitude, and such was the power attending the preached message that five thousand were converted. Stephen was 'full of faith and power'. Philip demonstrated God's power in Samaria while Peter received a fresh enduement in Cornelius' house. Lest we should regard this experience as the prerogative of the apostles and their immediate circle, the unnamed believers scattered by the persecution in Jerusalem were conscious that 'The hand of the Lord was with them, and a great number believed and turned to the Lord' (Acts 11:21). Paul and his companions knew the same *dunamis* in Philippi, Thessalonica, Corinth and Ephesus, and so on. Whatever may have been once-for-all about the beginning at Pentecost, it did not include the power which Jesus had promised. This was manifestly with those first preachers as they obeyed the Lord's command to go into all the world.

But some would have us believe this power ended with the apostolic age. The plain answer to that is that if that had been so the newborn church would have ended with it. This, of course, is not to suggest that the power once given is there and all that is needed is for us to plug into it. It is not my purpose to criticize, still less to ridicule, any fellow-Christian who takes this view, or alternately, the one that the power was intended only for the birth and the first generation of the Christian church, but I believe that the promise of our Lord in itself states otherwise and that New Testament records and the subsequent history of the church evince clear evidence that the Lord's promise, as well as his presence, was meant for as long as the work of the commission is to be done. That there have been periods when the power seemed to be withdrawn none can dispute: we believers of the twentieth century, with very few exceptions, are in one of those periods, much to our dismay. Some friends speak of 'power' for this, that and the other, but I know of no instance of the mighty power known at Pentecost being known in our time, with the gospel being proclaimed and thousands struck with the terror of law and of God and overwhelmed by the glories of Christ in salvation. There have been, and still are, drops of mercy for which we must all be thankful, but where are the showers? The work of the commission is to some degree continuing, both at home and abroad, and some power is attending it, for a trickle of souls are being saved and none is saved apart from that power. But the effusion that the Lord has given his people in former days is not now among us in these late years and both we and our gospel labours are grievously dry and fruitless.

The Lord is sovereign in the exercise of his power

The plain fact is that, while the Lord will never entirely withdraw his presence and power and leave his people as orphans, the effusions of both are subject to his gracious will and mercy. It was thus for his ancient people Israel and has been so for the Christian church and, though his will and purposes are past finding out, we can see good reason for it being so.

For one thing, had the outpouring at Pentecost continued unabated no human constitution could have borne the burden for long. Many, though not all, of the men who were involved in revival did not live to old age; Spurgeon died at fifty-eight, Whitefield at fifty-seven and Evan Roberts was a spent force at a comparatively young age. It is noteworthy that revival has often come with the ministry of young men — William Burns was twenty-four when the power fell on him in Kilsyth; Murray M'Cheyne was twenty-nine when he died after some years of revival in Dundee; Whitefield, Cennick, Harris, Rowland, Williams and many others were young men on whom the power fell in the eighteenth-century revival. In any case, were not the apostles young men too?

Then again, had the power been given once for all time, attempted manipulation of it would soon have followed by unspiritual people. Simon the sorcerer saw the power working in Samaria and offered a bribe, if only the apostles would give it to him. Equally if the power were available at all times, would it not soon have been taken for granted and encourage what has sometimes been called 'Finneyism', namely that we have only to do this or that and the power will come — power available on tap, as it were?

To permit his people to experience his presence and power in extraordinary measure is still the prerogative of the exalted Lord who works all things according to the counsel of his own will (Eph. 1:11). What is required of his people is that they should walk with him in humble obedience and do his work in accordance with his will as it is revealed in his Word. Their confidence is not to be in themselves, not in their own efforts, nor yet in the carnal ways of fallen humanity, but in the Lord who rules and reigns in all the affairs of his church. Most of all, the power is his to give or to withhold, that the glory may be his alone, for his is 'the kingdom, the power and the glory for ever, Amen'.

What about prayer? We are all familiar with praying for revival — all-night and half-night, early-morning and weekly prayer meetings have been held for many years, but still the blessing is withheld. If discouragement has set in, that is not surprising, but pray we must till the Lord will be entreated to pour out his grace and mercy upon us. Let our prayer, however, be for his glory and praise in the glorious fulfilment of his commission among us and in all the nations of the earth. 'You who make mention of the Lord, do not keep silent, and give him no rest till he establishes and till he makes Jerusalem a praise in the earth' (Isa. 62:6).

The power of God in revival

Nothing can be more comforting for us than to know that the one who commanded us to go, to preach and to witness, and who has come with such power upon his church at Pentecost and many times since, is 'the same yesterday, today and for ever'. We can work and pray and expect him to come once again to his people with an enduement of power that will change the face of Christianity in the world. If the latter is much disfigured in our day by unbelief, compromise and gross folly, this is only a repetition of what has happened many times since New Testament times. None of it withstood the power of God in revival and none will withstand it when he is pleased to visit us again.

Think of William Burns, a young preacher recently from college, announcing a Tuesday morning meeting at ten o'clock in Kilsyth to follow the communion weekend just ended and in which he had shared. He had 'exalted views of what might be expected even in these latter days [1839] from the outpouring of the Holy Spirit in answer to earnest prayer'. The words of Psalm 102:13 which were sung greatly impressed him: 'You will arise and have mercy on Zion; for the time to favour her, yes, the set time has come.' Preaching on 'Thy people shall be willing in the day of thy power' (Ps. 110:3, AV), he recalled the rain falling and the people putting on their coats as John Livingstone was ending his message in the open air at Kirk of Shotts in 1630. Livingstone had asked them if they had any covering to put on when the drops of God's wrath would fall. Exhorted to turn to the covering which is in Christ, over five hundred were converted. As Burns recounted the events of that day, weeping and crying broke out in the congregation and so great was the power that the service which started at ten in the morning went on till three in the afternoon and another was announced for six in the evening. What began that morning went on for weeks and was carried to many other parts of Scotland.

We can refer to another ten o'clock morning meeting held in front of the Red Lion Hotel at Llanidloes in mid-Wales in 1819. A large crowd was gathered for what was an Association meeting. The first preacher was Michael Roberts, aged twenty-six, whose text was Psalm 1:5: 'Therefore the ungodly shall not stand in the judgement, nor sinners in the congregation of the righteous.' Having described the judgement, he depicted the Judge's last word to the ungodly: 'Depart from me, ye cursed, into everlasting fire.' As Roberts cried out the judge's verdict people fell in an agony of guilt and despair; some wept while others forgot where they were standing. Ebenezer Morris, a renowned preacher, tried to follow Michael Roberts but failed and the meeting had to be closed.

Years later it was calculated that a thousand people had been added to the churches of Montgomeryshire in consequence of this one meeting in Llanidloes.

So many preachers in Wales knew the same mighty power for over a century, as did many others throughout Britain and the USA. The great George Whitefield experienced it in both countries for over thirty years, with great blessing following. Few scenes in church history can parallel those of Moorfields and Kennington Common in the eighteenth century when Whitefield preached to enormous crowds in the face of much opposition from various stall-holders whose trade was hindered. As he preached they pelted him with stones, dried cattle dung and pieces of dead cats, which were fielded by children endeavouring to protect the preacher.

A challenge to continued faithfulness

Two things characterized these men, and a multitude of others who could be cited: one is that they were preaching the gospel to every creature and freely calling sinners to believe in the Saviour — that is, they were doing what Christ in the Great Commission commanded us to do; the other is that the Lord kept his promise and came with exceptional heavenly power to make them and their labours fruitful. This is the pattern in the New Testament, it is the testimony of church history and it must be the concern of all believers still. Institutional churchianity, with its orders, forms, traditions and rites, does not know this power, and never will know it, for these outward forms have become ends in themselves. Revivals are for those whose allegiance is to him alone who told us that our chief business is to go into all the world and preach the gospel to every creature. We must accept no alternative, nor grow weary in the task. Still less can we be content with a jaded evangelicalism whose view of a lost world and of Christ and his salvation has become matter-of-fact and lukewarm.

When Savonarola's preaching broke upon Florence in pre-Reformation days the entire city-state was roused to the fear of God and concern of soul. The pope inevitably became alarmed and Savonarola was banned from preaching. He spent nearly a year in a monastery while his friends appealed to the pope for his reinstatement. They duly succeeded and Savonarola began preaching again, but found the Florentines had become offhand, though still gathering in large numbers to hear him. He told them that through the window of his room in the monastery he had seen a rook alighting on the bell-tower nearby. He knew the bell would soon be rung to call the monks to prayer and watched to see it dart away in fright at the loud clanging of the bell. A little later the rook returned and again Savonarola saw it fly away when the bell rang. But the bird liked the perch and continued to come back, 'And now', said Savonarola, 'it does not fly away any more!'

Can it be that we are like that rook? God forbid! It is time for us to pray and work as never before and to do so with our confidence solely in him who promised to be 'with you always, even to the end of the age'.

Appendix:
Notes of sermon preached by the author at the 1996 Aberystwyth conference

While we must believe that the Great Commission is relevant for the Christian church in every generation, it does not follow that every member of the church is commissioned to preach. On the contrary, while every Christian should be a witness, only those who are specifically called of God are required to preach — that is, to be public 'heralds' of the gospel, announcing and proclaiming it as those separated and endowed for that work.

We have only to look at those to whom the commission was first given to see that a few crucial facts were true of them. One was that *they had previously been called*. There were clearly many disciples who followed Jesus during his public ministry, but who were not called in the way and sense that the apostles were. The Gospels record that Jesus went out of his way to call the future preachers. 'He walked by the Sea of Galilee' and 'saw Simon and Andrew, his brother, casting a net into the sea... Then Jesus said to them, "Come after me, and I will make you become fishers of men"' (Mark 1:16-17).

The tendency to regard this as a mere incident in Christ's ministry and capable of general application is, I believe, most misleading. Certainly, Jesus by his Spirit calls sinners to himself and he saves those who are thus called and commands them to follow him. But among those thus called, saved and commanded to follow, Jesus still turns aside, as it were, and calls men to become preachers of the gospel.

But the men who first received the commission had already received something else. Having been called, *they were then taught the gospel*.

Even more, *they were entrusted with the gospel*, which became for them the 'burden of the Lord', a solemn trust which henceforth they would have to keep and discharge at whatever cost it might demand. In the words of the apostle Paul, 'Necessity is laid upon me, yea, woe is unto me, if I preach not the gospel!' (1 Cor. 9:16, AV). What was this necessity? It was the gospel which had been entrusted to him. He had received it from the Lord himself, as he tells the Galatians in chapter 1:12.

In my view being solemnly entrusted with the gospel is a profound aspect of the call to preach. Writing to the Romans, Paul said he had been 'separated to the gospel of God' (Rom. 1:1). He told the Galatians that he had been 'set apart from the womb', which I take to mean eternal election, and he was also 'called ... through ... grace, that I might preach him to the Gentiles' (Gal. 1:15,16). God calls a man to preach, and what he is to preach is entrusted to him in such a way as to displace every other interest and responsibility. The gospel becomes the essential of life itself, the consuming passion dominating mind, affections, will and time, as became evident in the lives of the first preachers and many who have followed them, forsaking families, friends and worldly benefits to live and die in lonely foreign fields. Well might we ask what ailed them? The plain answer is that God called them and put the gospel in their care to be taken and announced to men and women lost in sin, whatever this might demand of them.

Being trusted with this gospel becomes a compulsion — a necessity according to Paul — to preach what has been entrusted and our failure to do so results in 'Woe is to me!'

The *necessity* spoken of may have several connotations, but at root it expresses a factor which may be said to be endemic in gospel truth. If God 'so loved' the world that he gave his only Son', there was a 'necessity' on him, because of his infinite and ineffable love, to intervene definitively to save those whom he loved. And when he sent the Son he gave him the same 'necessity' to do what was required to save them. Under that compulsion 'he laid his glory by' and 'incomprehensibly was made man' to die the cursed death. Having accomplished all that the divine necessity involved, he called and entrusted men with the glad message and with that message comes the same necessity — that is, a divine constraint to announce the gospel to a lost world, whatever that may entail. Hence the endeavours of the apostles, heedless of enemies and physical demands, and hence the pioneer missionaries and the glorious martyrs, as well as the nameless witnesses who in hardship and loneliness have maintained the faith in unlikely situations. The whole of sacred history is packed with accounts of men who felt this same necessity. Noah certainly felt it as he built an ark in a desert of sand and preached righteousness for a century before the flood came. The three young men and Daniel knew it too as they defied pagan kings and power in the name of God. And it was the same 'necessity' which weighed on Martin Luther at the Diet of Worms when, against the threats of powerful enemies and the advice of supporters, he deliberately accepted the invitation to appear at the Diet with the words: 'I will enter Worms under the banner of Christ against the gates of hell.' What overpowered him as he stood before the Catholic emperor was the consciousness that both he and the emperor were called upon to answer before Almighty God. Twenty-four hours later he was saying before an overcrowded assembly which had required him to recant some of his writings, 'Unless I am convinced by Scripture and plain reason I do not accept the authority of popes and councils, for they have contradicted each other — my conscience is captive to the Word of God. I cannot, and I will not, recant anything, for to go against conscience is neither right nor safe. God help me. Amen. Here I stand. I cannot do otherwise.' Certainly this was that necessity which the apostle Paul expressed before King Agrippa: 'I was not disobedient to the heavenly vision' (Acts 26:19). The same compulsion was echoed by the pioneering preacher of Northampton, William Carey, who exclaimed, 'My business is the kingdom of God and I cobble shoes to pay the expenses,' and went on to master thirty or so languages in India.

'The love of Christ constrains us,' said Paul to the Corinthians (2 Cor. 5:14), which may well imply that the love of Christ in his death for sinners, which lay at the heart of the gospel entrusted to him, increased and enriched the necessity laid upon him by the call of God. This indeed was more than a call to office and function; it was rather a call which had a 'heart' in it — a constraint by Christ's love.

The story of John Williams of Erromanga is worth noting: being an engineer by profession he built himself a boat in which as a missionary he could reach the remote islands of Polynesia. Despite repeated warnings of danger he resolved to go to the island of Erromanga, whose natives were known cannibals. On disembarking from his boat he was killed on the beach. It was said that he had to go there because his heart had gone before him to the natives.

There is a heart in this necessity; Jeremiah and Paul suffered greatly because of it; so did the noble martyrs, and the same has been true of a host of men who, through hardship, unrelenting effort and great sacrifice, have preached the glad tidings of the gospel without fear or favour.

May this not be our crucial need at present — namely, a holy army of men whose preaching ministry is marked by this necessity?